Sarah M... ...erson.
Chattan +

A PONY CLUB PUBLICATION

The Pony Club Quiz Book

© 1985 The Pony Club
Reprinted 1989

Compiled by members of The Pony Club Training Committee

Design and illustrations by Victor Shreeve, with two
additional drawings by Joy Hawken

Published by The Pony Club

Designed, produced and distributed by
Threshold Books Limited, 661 Fulham Road, London SW6 5PZ

Printed in Great Britain by Westway Offset, Wembley

ISBN 0 900226 29 3

Introduction

This book of 1,000 questions has been produced by the Pony Club both to entertain and to instruct. It covers almost every aspect of the riding, care, and folklore of horses and ponies — though of course only a small proportion of the many thousands of possible questions could be included in one book.

All the questions in Part 1 can be answered correctly by anyone who has read and absorbed *The Manual of Horsemanship*, the Pony Club's official handbook. This section of the book is a useful revision for those taking efficiency tests, but it must be stressed that not all aspects of equitation and horsemastership can be covered by questions in a quiz. Memorising answers is no substitute for knowledge gained through practical experience.

Quiz masters at Pony Club branch and riding club competitions should find the book invaluable, and we hope that it will also provide hours of enjoyment for members, non-members, their families and friends.

CONTENTS

		question	page
(1)	**EQUITATION**	*1*	7
	HORSEMASTERSHIP AND STABLE-MANAGEMENT		
	The Grass-kept Pony	*101*	13
	Handling and Leading	*118*	14
	Stabling	*139*	15
	Clothing	*166*	16
	Grooming	*180*	17
	Clipping	*188*	17
	Feeding	*209*	18
	The Foot and Shoeing	*234*	19
	Health	*253*	20
	Exercise	*257*	21
	Competitions and Hunting	*266*	21
	Breeds, Colours, Age and Height	*275*	22
	Conformation	*312*	24
	Saddlery	*322*	24
	'CALL THE VET'	*377*	28
(2)	**THE PONY CLUB**	*445*	32
	Competitions and Championships	*491*	34
	Riding and Road Safety	*515*	35
	THE BRITISH HORSE SOCIETY	*535*	37
	The Law	*550*	38
	Affiliated Riding Clubs	*560*	39

3 **SPORTS AND PASTIMES**

Hunting	*569*	40
Horse Trials	*597*	43
Dressage	*613*	44
Show Jumping	*624*	45
Polo	*651*	46
Driving	*664*	47
Long Distance Riding	*677*	47
Showing	*685*	48
Racing	*697*	49

4 **SOME GENERAL QUESTIONS**

The 'Equine Connection'	*726*	52
Over the Seas and Far Away	*756*	53
Take Your Pick	*776*	54
A Visit to the Zoo?	*811*	59
Odd One Out	*841*	60
Double Meanings	*866*	61
Books, Poems and Pictures	*901*	62
The Numbers Game	*946*	65
The End of the Road	*961*	66

5 **SOME LOCAL QUESTIONS FOR QUIZ MASTERS** — *981* — 68

ANSWERS — 71

Equitation

1   Having saddled up your pony before mounting there are four final checks to make on the saddle. Name three of them.

2   Is there a correct side from which you should always mount? If so, which is it?

3   Before mounting, how do you check that your stirrup leathers are about the right length?

4   Before mounting, how do you check that your stirrup leathers are level?

5   When preparing to mount from the near side, where do you stand?

6   When preparing to mount, in which hand do you hold the reins?

7   How do you decide on the length of rein to use when mounting?

8   What is meant by 'giving a leg-up'?

9   If you cannot reach the stirrup with your foot, there are three ways of getting on. Give two of them.

10   You are mounted. Which is your pony's off-side?

11   You want to shorten your stirrups when mounted. What do you do —
    (a) With your feet?
    (b) With the reins?
    (c) With your whip?

12   You are riding with a single rein. Between which fingers should it pass?

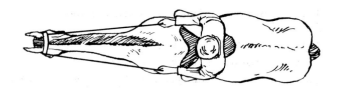

13 When holding the reins, your hands should form part of a straight line. Describe this line.

14 Name three natural aids.

15 Name two artificial aids.

16 If you are in the correct position in the saddle:
(a) In which part of the saddle should you be sitting?
(b) Which part of your foot should be resting on the stirrup iron?
(c) How much weight should be on the stirrup iron?

17 What do you do with your hands as the pony moves his head and neck at the walk?

18 Is there a correct side on which you should always dismount? If so, which is it?

19 When preparing to dismount what do you do:
(a) With your feet?
(b) With your reins?
(c) With your whip?

20 You praise and encourage your pony with your voice. Give two other reasons for using the voice.

21 Which two factors influence the length of stirrup that you use?

22 Which stage should your riding reach before you can use spurs?

23 At rising trot how do you know if you are on the left diagonal?

24 At rising trot how do you change diagonal?

25 On which occasions should you change diagonal at the trot?

26 On which diagonal should you ride when at rising trot in a manège?

27 At which stage of rising trot should most weight be placed on the stirrup irons?

28 In rising trot should your body be:
(a) Upright?
(b) Inclined forward?
(c) Leaning slightly back?

29 Where should the rider look when circling?

30 In which hand should you normally hold the whip when schooling?

31 A pony's paces are in two, three or four times, according to the number of beats in each stride. In what time are:
(a) Walk?
(b) Trot?
(c) Canter?
(d) Gallop?

32 What is the sequence of footfalls in the walk, starting with the near hind?

33 At which pace do a pony's two diagonal pairs of feet move alternately?

34 How should the rider use the outside leg when giving the aid to canter?

35 Why are spurs used?

36 When galloping, where should the rider's weight be?

37 How do too short leathers affect your position in the saddle?

38 If your leathers are too long, how may your position in rising trot be affected?

39 What adjustment should you make to your stirrup leathers before jumping?

40 What additional piece of saddlery should a novice rider use when jumping?

41 An analysis of a pony's jump divides it into five phases. Name them in sequence.

42 On which phase does the success of the jump largely depend?

43 Why is holding on to the mane when jumping a bad habit to acquire?

44 For how many strides before a jump must a pony be allowed to concentrate on the jump without undue interference from the rider?

45 When jumping, a pony lowers his head just before take-off. What does he do with his head and neck *on* take-off?

46 Why should you never pile cavaletti on top of each other to make a jump?

47 What is a false ground line?

48 In a course of jumps what is a double?

49 If a horse refuses at a schooling fence through lack of confidence, what immediate action do you take?

50 Give three reasons why a well-ridden pony might refuse or run out.

51 What term describes the mistake of asking a pony to jump beyond his ability?

52 Why should you not walk over closely placed trotting poles?

53 Why should you never trot over two poles placed 4½ feet apart?

54 Why should rising trot normally be used over trotting poles?

55 Where should the hind feet fall in relation to trotting poles?

56 What pace should be used when first teaching a horse to negotiate a pole on the ground?

57 What would be about the correct distance between each trotting pole for a horse?

58 Give three 'ingredients' of an inviting fence.

59 There are four basic types of fence. Name them.

60 What name is given to a fence where a horse lands over the first element and takes off for the second with no non-jumping stride between them?

61 How many poles should be used on the last element of a parallel fence?

62 Why do crossed poles make a useful schooling fence?

63 Why should you trot rather than canter in the early stages of teaching a young horse to jump?

64 Name three different walks.

65 When the horse is moving on a curve where should the footprint of the outside hind foot fall?

66 Which of the rider's legs asks for impulsion, and how?

67 Which hand:
(a) Regulates the speed and pace?
(b) Allows and controls the bend?
(c) Asks for direction?

68 In which time is rein-back?

69 What is the sequence of steps in rein-back?

70 What is the basic difference between the aids for the walk and the aids for the rein-back?

71 What should the rider's reaction be when the leg-aid, correctly applied, is disobeyed?

72 What term is used to describe a fast and hurried trot?

73 Which are the three most common faults in extended trot?

74 Name four different canters.

75 What is the sequence of footfalls in the canter, off-fore leading?

76 What is meant by cantering 'disunited'?

77 What is the consequence of riding with a stiff back while cantering?

78 What are the two most common faults in medium canter?

79 What is a period of suspension?

80 At which paces is there a period of suspension?

81 How should the horse's weight be distributed at the halt?

82 Which of the following describe a correct, and which an incorrect, outline:
(a) The poll as the highest point?
(b) The front of the face just behind the vertical?
(c) The back supple and relaxed?
(d) The tail swinging?
(e) The jaw relaxed?
(f) The hind legs kept low and dwelling on the ground?

83 What term is used to describe the energy supplied by the horse when asked for by the rider?

84 How is the regularity and evenness of the hoofbeats described in one word?

85 Through how many degrees is a demi-pirouette performed?

86 At which paces can the pirouette be carried out?

87 What is the function of the rider's inside leg in the pirouette?

88 At which pace is leg-yielding usually carried out?

89 In which of the following movements is the horse bent in the direction in which he is travelling:
(a) Leg-yielding?
(b) Shoulder-in?
(c) Half-pass?
(d) Pirouette?

90 Is shoulder-in performed on two, three or four tracks?

91 What is 'tracking-up'?

92 In which of the following paces does the horse overtrack:
(a) Collected walk?
(b) Medium walk?
(c) Extended walk?

93 Why should turns on the forehand not be carried out too often?

94 Which of the following movements can be attempted with only a slight degree of collection having been achieved:
(a) Turn on the forehand?
(b) Shoulder-in?
(c) Leg-yielding?
(d) Demi-pirouette?

95 What is the maximum angle that the horse's body should make with the track in shoulder-in?

96 On which rein should right shoulder-in be performed:
(a) Right rein?
(b) Left rein?
(c) Either rein?

97 What is the effect on the horse's shoulders of too much bend in half-pass?

98 What is the pace between collected and medium trot called?

99 Give four reasons why trotting poles are of value to the rider.

100 Why should a bounce fence never be at the end of a gymnastic line for a young horse?

HORSEMASTERSHIP AND STABLE MANAGEMENT

The Grass-kept Pony

101 Over which months can grass form the main part of a pony's diet?

102 At what time of year does a grass-kept pony need extra feed?

103 How often should a pony at grass be visited?

104 Why is too much rich spring grass dangerous to ponies?

105 If there is not a shelter shed in the field, what alternative should be provided for a pony turned out in summer?

106 Why is a grass-kept pony less susceptible to injury to his wind and limb than one which is stabled?

107 Why should a grass-kept pony be groomed less thoroughly than one which is stabled?

108 Why should an unclipped pony at grass be turned out immediately after exercise?

109 Is it most important to provide shelter from (a) rain? (b) snow? (c) wind?

110 When do ponies make most use of a field shelter, and why?

111 Why should you leave the cobwebs in a shelter shed?

112 Why is a circular shed suitable as a field shelter?

113 If a pony spends part of the time stabled and part at grass, when should he be turned out?

114 Which is the most suitable type of paddock fencing?

115 How high should the lowest strand of a plain wire fence be?

116 What is the bare minimum acreage for one pony which is kept at grass throughout the year?

117 What type of rug should be worn by a pony at grass?

Handling and Leading

118 How do you reassure a pony as you approach him?

119 What part of the pony should you approach?

120 Where and how should you first touch a pony on approaching him?

121 Of what material is a headcollar usually made?

122 Of what material is a halter usually made?

123 To which 'D' on the headcollar should the rope be fastened?

124 When lifting a foreleg which way should you face?

125 When holding up a foreleg, by which part should you hold it?

126 Where do you walk in relation to your pony when leading him?

127 How should you hold the headrope when leading?

128 What should you use to lead a pony on or near a public road?

129 In which direction should you turn a led pony?

130 Is there a correct side from which to lead a pony when not on a road? Which is it?

131 There are four ways of using the reins of a snaffle bridle to lead a pony. Name three of them.

132 When riding and leading a fresh pony, should the led pony's head be —
(a) Level with the ridden pony's?
(b) Level with your knee?
(c) Level with the ridden pony's quarters?

133 Which are the two ways of securing the reins on a led pony if you are not using them for leading?

134 What do you do with the running martingale on a led pony?

135 What is meant by 'running-up in hand'?

136 When showing off a pony at the halt where should you stand and how should you hold him?

137 From which side do you lead a pony on the public highway?

138 What should you do if a pony you are leading in hand will not move forward?

Stabling

139 Why is a stable door made in two halves?

140 How many latches are needed on the bottom half of a stable door?

141 Give three reasons why a grill is placed over the top half of a stable door.

142 What is the minimum width for a stable door?

143 Why should a stable door open outwards?

144 Name three disadvantages of stalls.

145 What governs the height of a swinging bale used as a stall division?

146 What are the characteristics of a good stable floor?

147 How should drainage be provided?

148 Ventilation should provide plenty of air. What should be avoided?

149 What is an essential fitting in any stable?

150 What further fittings may be provided in a loosebox?

151 At what height should a manger be fitted?

152 Where should a stable electric light switch be positioned?

153 When securing a pony by log and rope, what determines the length of the rope?

154 Give three reasons why bedding is provided in a stable.

155 Which straw is best for bedding?

156 What is to 'set fair'?

157 What are the disadvantages of barley straw as bedding?

158 What can be done to prevent a pony from eating straw bedding?

159 How often should droppings be removed?

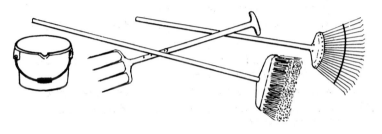

160 How often should a deep litter bed be renewed?

161 What is the term used for tying a horse by a short rope to a high ring when grooming?

162 How high should this ring be placed?

163 If manure is put out to rot, how many heaps are needed and for what purpose?

164 How would you set about getting a horse out of a stable which is on fire?

165 Beyond the danger of getting burned or trapped, what is particularly hazardous about fire for horses?

Clothing

166 What clothing is used to keep a stabled horse warm?

167 What clothing is available —
(a) For an overheated horse?
(b) On a wet day at a show?
(c) On a hot dusty day at a show?

168 What do you call a leather or webbing 'girth' which is padded to keep pressure off the spine and used to keep clothing in place?

169 What are the characteristics of a New Zealand rug?

170 What is the string which fastens across the back of a day rug called?

171 Why are stable bandages used?

172 What is the usual width of a stable bandage?

173 Which of the following materials are suitable for stable bandages —
(a) Stockinette?
(b) Wool?
(c) Crepe?
(d) Elastic synthetic?

174 What should be used under a stable bandage to avoid undue or uneven pressure?

175 Why should the tapes of a stable bandage be fastened at the side?

176 How should an exercise bandage be secured before riding a cross-country course?

177 Why should a tail bandage not be left on at night?

178 How should water be used when applying a tail bandage?

179 List as many different horse boots as you can.

Grooming

180 Name three different brushes used for grooming.

181 What is a metal curry-comb used for?

182 What is used to polish the coat?

183 What name is given to a massage pad of hay or straw?

184 Which brush should be used on the mane and tail?

185 Which parts of the body should be given special attention with the dandy brush?

186 How do you check the shoes when picking out the feet?

187 How long will an experienced groom take to groom a horse?

Clipping

188 Give four reasons for clipping.

189 In what condition should a horse's coat be before clipping?

190 Where should clipping be started on a nervous horse?

191 Which parts of a horse are particularly difficult to clip?

192 From which part should the hair never be removed?

193 What is a 'hunter clip'?

194 What is a 'blanket clip'?

195 Which clips are suitable for grass-kept ponies?

196 Why are the legs left unclipped in a hunter clip?

197 How do you compensate for loss of the coat of a clipped-out stabled horse?

198 At what stage should the first winter clip be done?

199 When should the last clip of the winter be done?

200 When is the easiest time to pull mane and tail?

201 What should be done periodically while using electric clippers?

202 What is 'hogging'?

203 What is the minimum number of plaits for a hunter?

204 Name two ways of securing mane plaits.

205 Why should mane plaits not be left in overnight?

206 What name is given to a tail with the end cut square?

207 What name is given to a tail pulled to a point?

208 Why does 'no horse look good at blackberry time'?

Feeding

209 Which is the best grain for feeding to horses?

210 Why should this grain be fed sparingly to most ponies?

211 How soon may a pony be worked after a normal feed?

212 How soon may a pony be worked hard after a full drink?

213 What is a 'bad-doer'?

214 What is a 'shy-feeder'?

215 Which by-product of sugar manufacture can be used to tempt shy-feeders?

216 How long should barley be boiled before feeding?

217 What is a 'wasteful feeder'?

218 Give three ways of preventing a horse from being wasteful.

219 What must be well soaked before feeding?

220 Which is the one form in which wheat is suitable for feeding?

221 How long can crushed oats be kept before they deteriorate?

222 How does barley compare with oats as a feed?

223 Why should root vegetables be sliced lengthwise before feeding?

224 How long should hay be stored before feeding?

225 How should loose hay be fed to ponies at grass?

226 What are the two main types of hay?

227 What is the rough relationship between quantity of feed and bodyweight — (a) $\frac{1}{30}$ (b) $\frac{1}{40}$ (c) $\frac{1}{50}$?

228 As a rough guide, what is the total weight of feed needed daily by a 16-hand horse?

229 What is the least number of times a stabled horse should be fed daily?

230 At what height should a haynet be hung in stable or shelter?

231 What is chaff?

232 How often should water troughs be attended to in frosty weather?

233 How is sand colic commonly caused?

The Foot and Shoeing

234 Name those parts of the foot visible on the underside of a shod hoof.

235 Which part of the foot absorbs concussion and prevents slipping?

236 From where does the wall of the hoof grow?

237 Give four reasons for re-shoeing.

238 What is the removal and replacement of a shoe called?

239 What does 'casting' a shoe mean?

240 What is a clench?

241 How many clips are usual on fore and on hind shoes?

242 What is a 'buffer'?

243 What are the two systems of shoeing?

244 Which of these two systems is most satisfactory, and why?

245 What is a 'nail-bind'?

246 When is a horse 'pricked'?

247 What is 'dumping'?

248 What term is used to describe a nail not driven far enough into the wall to secure the shoe?

249 What name is given to the groove on the ground surface of a shoe which improves the grip on grass?

250 For what purpose is a feather-edged shoe fitted?

251 What name is given to a thin half-shoe fitted to horses at grass?

252 What attention do unshod feed need from the farrier?

Health

253 What are the signs of good health seen in —
(a) The ears?
(b) The coat?
(c) The skin?
(d) The eyes and nostrils?

254 How many inhalations per minute should a healthy horse make while at rest?

255 What is the body temperature of a healthy horse?

256 What is the pulse rate of a healthy horse?

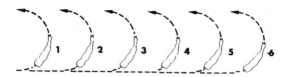

Exercise

257 What is the one aspect of a horse's life in which he benefits from a varied routine?

258 Give three reasons why you might lunge a horse for exercise.

259 List the lungeing equipment needed for a horse.

260 Which of the following should be worn when lungeing — (*a*) hard hat, (*b*) gloves, (*c*) spurs?

261 Which three aids are used to control a horse on the lunge?

262 How should the voice be used for transitions increasing the pace?

263 How should the handler move while lungeing?

264 Give two methods of halting a horse who will not obey the command to halt on the lunge?

265 Once a horse is in hard condition, how are the back and girth regions kept hard?

Competitions and Hunting

266 At what speed should you plan to hack a grass-kept pony to an event or meet?

267 At what speed should you plan to hack a stable-kept horse to an event or meet?

268 What is the ideal distance from the meet at which to un-box?

269 What does a red tail ribbon mean?

270 What does a green tail ribbon mean?

271 What privileges does a red tail ribbon entitle you to?

272 How should water be offered to a tired horse after a long day?

273 What can you tell by feeling a horse's ears in the stable?

274 What routine should you follow for a stabled horse the day after very hard work, such as horse trials or hunting?

Breeds, Colours, Age and Height.

275 Name the nine breeds of ponies native to the United Kingdom.

276 What breed of horse is recorded in the General Stud Book?

277 What term describes a horse with one parent in the General Stud Book?

278 What proof is needed to show that a horse or pony belongs to a particular breed?

279 Which of the following are recognised breeds —
(*a*) Cleveland Bay?
(*b*) Hackney ?
(*c*) Hunter ?
(*d*) Polo pony ?
(*e*) Anglo-Arab?

280 Which are the 'points' which decide the colour of a horse?

281 How do you distinguish between a brown horse and a bay of similar body colour?

282 What is the dark line along the back of a dun called?

283 What are the variations of the colour chestnut?

284 What are the three variations of roan?

285 Name the colour of a pony with irregular patches of black and white.

286 Name the colour when the irregular patches are white and a colour other than black.

287 What colour is a grey horse in whose coat black hairs predominate?

288 What is a white patch of hairs on the forehead called?

289 What is a narrow white mark down the face called?

290 Name the white mark between the nostrils.

291 Name the broad white mark down the face and over the nose.

292 What is an eye with white or blue-white colouring called?

293 How can a horse's age be determined?

294 What are the first set of teeth grown by a foal called?

295 By what age does a colt grow his first permanent teeth?

296 At what age is a horse said to have a full-mouth?

297 When does a hook appear on the top corner tooth?

298 When does this hook disappear?

299 What is the official birthday of all Thoroughbreds?

300 What part of a horse is used to determine his height?

301 What is the unit of measurement used?

302 What unit of measurement is used for Shetland ponies?

303 How many inches are there in a hand?

304 Under what scheme are widely accepted measurement certificates provided?

305 Who may measure for a height certificate?

306 What three conditions must be fulfilled for accurate measurement?

307 How are the shoes taken into account when measuring?

308 What three useful purposes are served by knowing a horse's height?

309 Name the three terms used for —
(*a*) A pony in his first year.
(*b*) A pony in the year after the year of birth.
(*c*) A female pony up to 3 years old.
(*d*) A female of any age.
(*e*) A castrated male.

310 What is a cross between a donkey stallion and a pony mare?

311 What is a cross between a stallion and a she-ass?

Conformation

312 What is the term which describes narrow, donkey-like feet?

313 What is the usual angle between the wall of a normal foot and the ground?

314 What injury is likely to occur with feet that turn outwards?

315 What faulty action comes from toes that turn in?

316 What are the likely consequences of a head set at too acute an angle to the neck?

317 What is a convex face-line called?

318 If the ears are frequently laid back what temperament does this often indicate?

319 What sort of temperament is associated with —
(*a*) Showing a lot of white of the eye?
(*b*) Small, deeply set eyes?

320 What describes a horse with a measurement below the knee which is smaller than that lower down the cannon bone?

321 Where would you place yourself to see whether a horse has a curb?

Saddlery

322 What is the stable term for all saddlery?

323 What is the purpose of a saddle?

324 How do you measure a saddle to find its size?

325 What is fastened to the back of a saddle to stop it from slipping forward?

326 What alteration to a saddle will help to prevent it slipping forward on a fat horse or one with low withers?

327 If the cantle can be bent backwards and forwards, what do you suspect?

328 If a saddle slopes backwards, what is likely to be wrong?

329 When buying a second-hand saddle what is the most important part to inspect?

330 For what purposes is a numnah used?

331 What materials are used to make girths?

332 What are Balding and Atherstone girths made of?

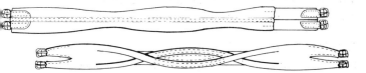

333 To which of the three straps on a saddle should the two buckles of a girth be fastened?

334 How would you keep a threefold girth soft and pliable?

335 Why should small children never use adult stirrup irons?

336 How can a saddle without stirrup bars be made safe?

337 In what position should the clips at the end of the stirrup bars be when riding?

338 What is the strongest and safest metal for bits and stirrup irons?

339 When fitting a stirrup, what should be the gap on either side of the foot?

340 Name three different types of leather which are used to make stirrup leathers.

341 Stirrup leathers stretch. What should you check from time to time?

342 How do you prevent the most used parts of stirrup leathers from getting badly worn?

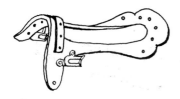

343 What are the three standard sizes of bridle?

344 What part of the bridle joins the headpiece to the bit?

345 What part of the bridle prevents the headpiece from slipping backwards?

346 How tightly should the throat lash be adjusted?

347 How tightly should the cavesson noseband be adjusted?

348 Give two uses of the lipstrap.

349 What different materials are used to make reins?

350 How does the bridoon rein differ from the bit rein on a double bridle?

351 To which rein on a double bridle is a running martingale attached?

352 What is the purpose of an Irish martingale?

353 Which two parts of the horse must not be restricted when a breast girth is correctly fitted?

354 What are the three main types of bit?

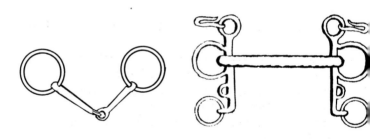

355 What standard of measurement is used for bits? What are the smallest and largest sizes?

356 How can you tell whether a bit fits?

357 On what part of the mouth does the bit rest?

358 Name five parts of the mouth and head on which the bit, with related parts of the bridle, acts.

359 On what parts of the head do bits with long cheek-pieces exert extra pressure?

360 On what part of the mouth does a 'port' act?

361 On what part of the mouth does the centre plate of a Dr Bristol act?

362 What is the function of a 'tongue groove'?

363 On what part of the head does the hackamore exert pressure?

364 With which bits may a drop noseband be fitted?

365 In which circumstances does a horse feel pressure on the nose from a drop noseband?

366 How high above the nostril should the front of a drop noseband be adjusted?

367 To which pieces of saddlery are the ends of a standing martingale attached?

368 Which of the following should never be used on leather —
(a) Neatsfoot oil?
(b) Soda?
(c) Detergent?
(d) Hot water?
(e) Dubbin?

369 Why should you not use neatsfoot oil on the seat of the saddle?

370 What should be the temperature of water used for cleaning tack?

371 Name the wooden structure on which a saddle is rested for cleaning.

372 What is wrong if saddle soap lathers on the sponge?

373 How should out-of-use saddlery be stored?

374 Which part of any piece of leather saddlery needs the most careful inspection for signs of wear?

375 What signs of deterioration would you look for when examining a bit?

376 Which articles of grooming kit are also used for cleaning tack?

'CALL THE VET'

Some questions on Health, Sickness and Injury.

377 Do the following indicate good or ill health?
    (a) A glossy coat.
    (b) Ribs easily visible.
    (c) A forefoot resting.
    (d) A hindfoot resting.
    (e) Limbs smooth and cool to touch.
    (f) Strong smelling droppings.
    (g) One foot warm to the touch.

378 About how many droppings should a healthy pony make in 24 hours?

379 How often should a pony's teeth be inspected for sharpness?

380 What name is given to small, late-developing teeth in front of the top molars, which can cause great discomfort?

381 For what purpose should you dose a pony at regular intervals?

382 List six of the nine items which should be in a travelling first-aid box.

383 Where are the three places for feeling the pulse?

384 With what part of your hand should you feel the pulse?

385 On what occasions should you call a vet?

386 What general preparation should you make for the vet's visit?

387 How would you secure a horse which the vet says is not to be allowed to lie down?

388 What is the normal diet for a sick horse confined to its box?

389 Which foods must be avoided when a horse is confined to its box?

390 If it is necessary to isolate a horse, what steps should you take to prevent the spread of infection?

391 How often should you offer food to a horse which is reluctant to eat?

392 If the vet gives you a powder to administer to your horse, in what different ways might you give it?

393 For ponies kept at grass, what injuries and infections can usually be treated in the field?

394 When must a sick grass-kept pony be brought into the stable?

395 How often should you visit a sick pony at grass?

396 How can a horse be prevented from tearing off dressings?

397 How should you prepare a horse's leg for cold hosing?

398 For how many minutes should you cold hose a leg?

399 What is the difference between hot fomentation and hot tubbing?

400 Give three reasons for poulticing.

401 What are the five main types of wound?

402 What are the four principal stages in treating a wound?

403 What is a simple method of stopping arterial bleeding by pressure while out on a hack?

404 What injuries can be caused by an ill-fitting saddle and a loose girth?

405 What is a form of ringworm caught from an infected girth?

406 What do you call an area of dead skin caused by saddle pressure?

407 How would you treat a mouth injury caused by an ill-fitting bit?

408 What is the result of failing to dry the heels after work?

409 If in winter the skin of the legs and stomach become tender and scaly, what is likely to be wrong with the pony?

410 What is the wound called when a hind shoe cuts the bulb of the front heel?

411 In what part of the horse does lameness mostly occur?

412 What should be the first action of a rider who suddenly feels his pony going unevenly?

413 From what disease of the foot are fat, under-exercised ponies likely to suffer?

414 What disease of the foot would you suspect if a horse was very lame in front on leaving the stable, but gradually became sound?

415 What offensive-smelling disease of the foot is caused by neglect?

416 What do you call an arthritic condition of the pedal bone?

417 What do you call a crack in the wall of the hoof starting at the coronet?

418 When a horse is being treated for lameness in one leg, should anything be done to the opposite, sound leg?

419 Where would you look for thoroughpin?

420 What is a bony enlargement of the pastern bones?

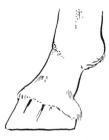 

421 What is a small bony knob usually forming on the inside of a foreleg below the knee?

422 What are the three main types of cough?

423 What steps can be taken to prevent a horse catching equine influenza?

424 An abcess in the jowl region and profuse nasal catarrh are symptoms of which contagious disease?

425 What steps should be taken to prevent tetanus?

426 What part of the breathing system is damaged in —
(a) Broken wind?
(b) Roaring?

427 What are the two operations used in cases of roaring and whistling?

428 What is the irritation called which causes a horse to rub areas of the mane and tail bare?

429 What contagious skin condition leaves small circular patches of bare skin?

430 On which parts of the horse are the two common species of lice found?

431 What steps should be taken to prevent reinfection or the spread of contagious disease after a cure has been effected?

432 How should the temperature of a hot poultice be tested before it is applied?

433 For how long should a limb be immersed when hot tubbing?

434 What should be added to water used for hot fomentation?

435 How many pieces of towelling are needed for hot fomentation?

436 How long should a poultice be left in place?

437 What item of forage is used as a poultice?

438 To which ailment are horses with flat thin soles prone?

439 What should be your first action if your horse refuses his feed and appears dull and listless?

440 How long will a severely blistered horse be off work?

441 What would you suspect if your horse was restless, breathing heavily, and looking round at his flank?

442 What should you never do to a wound close to a joint?

443 What is usually indicated by soil-licking and bark-gnawing?

444 What special attention do old horses need?

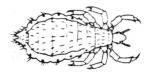

THE PONY CLUB

445 What is the minimum age for membership of the Pony Club?

446 What is the maximum age for membership of the Pony Club?

447 What are the two classes of members?

448 How many branches can a member belong to?

449 On joining, two fees must be paid. What are they for?

450 On what date is the annual subscription due?

451 By what date must the annual subscription be paid to avoid possible termination of membership?

452 At what age can an ordinary member apply to become an Associate?

453 In which annual publication are the Pony Club rules printed?

454 Where is the headquarters of the Pony Club?

455 What is the official title of the head of a branch?

456 To whom is the head of the branch responsible?

457 What is the minimum number of persons needed to form a branch local committee?

458 Branches are grouped into Areas. What is the title of the person responsible for an Area?

459 Into how many Areas is the Pony Club divided in the United Kingdom?

460 Who elects the Area Representative?

461 To which higher body is the Pony Club Council responsible?

462 What is the composition of the Pony Club Council?

463 What is 'The Backbone of the Pony Club'?

464 Which ponies are unacceptable at rallies?

465 Why are plimsols and heelless boots unsafe?

466 What type of spurs are permitted at rallies?

467 How can a member attend working rallies of another branch?

468 Which article of clothing is obligatory for all mounted rallies?

469 When may a member ride again after being concussed at a rally?

470 What are the six standards of efficiency?

471 There are seven colours denoting standards of efficiency. Why is there one more than the number of standards?

472 What are the seven colours which may be worn behind the badge and what does each mean?

473 Who signs efficiency certificates?

474 Which certificates may be awarded before the member has passed the Riding and Road Safety test?

475 Which test cannot be taken until the previous test has been passed?

476 Which certificates are awarded other than the efficiency standards?

477 Who may examine the 'C' Test?

478 Who may examine the 'A' Test?

479 What period must elapse before a failed candidate may retake the 'B' Test?

480 What are the Pony Club colours?

481 What are the colours of the Pony Club badge?

482 What is the title of the official handbook of the Pony Club?

483 In which year was the Pony Club formed?

484 Name two of the first seven branches which were formed.

485 Four countries overseas have over 100 Pony Club branches. Can you name two of them?

486 What are the qualifications for applicants for a Pony Club scholarship?

487 What do the initials VI stand for?

488 Who must countersign the entry form for a competition run by another branch?

489 What is the maximum prize money which may be given at a Pony Club competition?

490 What is the official colour of a first rosette?

Competitions and Championships

491 What form did the first ever Inter-Branch Competition take?

492 Name the six inter-branch championships.

493 Which inter-branch championships include no individual awards?

494 In which championships are the following trophies awarded —
(a) The Jack Gannon trophy?
(b) The Prince Philip Cup?
(c) The Greatheart Challenge Cup?
(d) The Dame Mary Colvin Challenge Cup?

495 In which year was a horse trials competition first held between branches of the Pony Club?

496 What are the phases of a Pony Club one-day horse trial?

497 Which phase always takes place first?

498 Which Pony Club branch has won the Horse Trials Team Championship and the junior individual award in the same three successive years?

499 When was the Prince Philip Cup first competed for?

500 What is the age limit for Prince Philip Cup teams?

501 What is the height limit for Prince Philip Cup team ponies?

502 How many members are there in a Prince Philip Cup team?

503 Where are the finals of the Prince Philip Cup held?

504 When was the first Pony Club Polo Championship held?

505 Name the three different competitions within the Polo Championships.

506 In which year was the first Inter-Branch Tetrathlon competition held?

507 In what fundamental way do the teams for tetrathlon differ from those for the other inter-branch competitions?

508 For whom were the early tetrathlon championships devised?

509 What different phases are there in the tetrathlon?

510 In which of these phases is there a highest possible score which cannot be bettered?

511 When were the first Pony Club Show Jumping Championships held?

512 How many members are there in a branch show jumping team?

513 Under what BSJA table is the Inter-Branch Show Jumping Competition judged?

514 In which year was the first Pony Club Team Dressage Championship held?

Riding and Road Safety

515 Whose instructions must you obey when riding on the road?

516 Which of the following must you conform to when riding on the roads —
(a) The Highway Code?
(b) Traffic signs?
(c) Traffic lights?
(d) Pedestrian-controlled lights?

517 What safety precautions should you take if you are riding on the roads after lighting-up time?

518 On which side of the road should you ride?

519 On which side of the road should you lead a pony?

520 If you arrive at a level crossing which has no gates, how will you know if a train is coming?

521 When can you safely cross an unguarded level crossing?

522 Would you take any action before passing another rider whom you had caught up?

523 If you are riding in a group, how many riders should ride abreast?

524 If your pony will not stand quietly, how should you approach a road junction?

525 Why should you take special care when trotting around corners?

526 If you were on your own and your pony would not pass a hazard, what would you do?

527 If you have to ride on an icy road, on which part of the road should you ride?

528 If the road is very slippery, what precautions should you take?

529 If you have to ride in snow, what can you do to prevent snow packing into balls in your pony's feet?

530 How should you protect yourself against a claim arising from an accident in which your pony may cause harm to others?

531 If you are involved in an accident, what should you record at the time?

532 What should you be careful never to say after an accident?

533 Are you entitled to ride your pony on —
(*a*) A bridleway?
(*b*) Public roads other than motorways?
(*c*) Motorways?
(*d*) The grass verge beside a motor road?
(*e*) Footpaths and pavements?

534 What should every rider always do when another road-user shows them consideration?

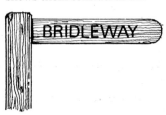

THE BRITISH HORSE SOCIETY

535 What do the following initials stand for —
(a) BHS?
(b) FBHS?
(c) BHSI?
(d) BHSII?
(e) BHSAI?

536 Where is the headquarters of the BHS?

537 When was the BHS founded?

538 Which bodies amalgamated to form the BHS?

539 How is the BHS organised throughout the United Kingdom?

540 What are the three main aspects of the Society's work which are represented by regional officers throughout the country?

541 Which competitions are controlled by committees within the BHS?

542 Which of the following are subordinate to the BHS —
(a) British Show Jumping Association?
(b) Horse and Pony Breeds Committee?
(c) The National Pony Society?
(d) Riding for the Disabled Association?
(e) The Pony Club?

543 How would you know where to find a riding school offering sound riding instruction?

544 What approval is needed before a riding establishment is allowed to offer horses for hire?

545 How would you know where to obtain riding instruction of a particular type or standard?

546 If you are interested in trekking or trail riding how would you set about finding a suitable establishment?

547 What must you join before you can compete in BHS affiliated competitions?

548 Which organisation brings together the common interests of the BHS and the BSJA?

549 Which major horse show is organised by the BHS?

The Law

550 Which horses must by law be partitioned away from other horses while in transit?

551 Horses may not be transported in the same vehicle as pigs, but there is an exception. Do you know what it is?

552 How often must horses be fed whilst in transit?

553 What is the minimum headroom allowed in a vehicle for transporting horses?

554 Under what act is cruelty to horses forbidden?

555 If you believe that a horse or pony is being cruelly treated or neglected, who should you inform?

556 How is the welfare of horses at sales regulated?

557 Where would you find a map of local bridleways?

558 Which of the following require planning permission —
(a) Grazing land for horses and ponies?
(b) An all weather outdoor arena?
(c) A covered school?
(d) A loosebox and tackroom?
(e) A field shelter?

559 Which of the following are required by law to be licensed annually by the local authority —
(a) A livery yard?
(b) Any establishment training clients on their own horses?
(c) An establishment which hires out donkeys?

Affiliated Riding Clubs

560 When were Riding Clubs first affiliated to the BHS?

561 What is the minimum age for adult membership of a Riding Club?

562 In what circumstances is membership allowed below this age?

563 What are the tests which Riding Club members may take?

564 Holders of certain Pony Club efficiency certificates are exempt from taking some Riding Club tests. Which certificates relate to which tests?

565 What is the title of the Riding Club test which may be taken by junior members?

566 What merit tests may be taken by junior members?

567 What are the six competitions which culminate in Riding Club Championships?

568 What are the two annual Riding Club team competitions with finals at the Royal International Horse Show and the Horse of the Year Show?

SPORTS AND PASTIMES

Hunting

569 Which is the traditional day for the start of the foxhunting season?

570 What is the collective term for people who ride to hounds?

571 Who controls these people?

572 How are hounds counted?

573 What is the 'Cap' (other than headgear)?

574 Who must you greet when arriving at the meet, and what do you say?

575 The following terms are used in the hunting field. What do they mean:
(*a*) Covert (pronounced 'cover')?
(*b*) The 'line' of a fox?
(*c*) A 'cold' line?
(*d*) A 'heel' line?
(*e*) A 'headed' fox?
(*f*) A 'sinking' fox?
(*g*) Mask?
(*h*) Brush?
(*i*) Pad?
(*j*) Brace?
(*k*) Earth?

576 What terms are used for the following:
(a) A hound's tail?
(b) Two leather hound-collars joined by a short chain?
(c) The place where hounds and hunt staff live?
(d) The 'rooms' in which hounds live?
(e) The raised platforms on which hounds sleep?
(f) An enclosed area where hounds can be in the open air and are fed?
(g) Reporting 'All hounds present' when out hunting or exercising?

577 Name two types of hound which hunt hares.

578 What is meant by:
(a) Hound music?
(b) Hounds singing?
(c) Hounds marking?

579 Why does the huntsman blow his horn?

580 What is:
(a) A 'check'?
(b) 'Riot'?
(c) 'Foil'?
(d) To 'chop'?
(e) 'Straight necked'?

581 What is the warning cry to indicate that a fence is unsafe to jump because there is wire in it?

582 What is a 'holloa' (pronounced holler)?

583 What are the huntsman's assistants called?

584 What are 'seeds'?

585 What is:
(a) A Lawn Meet?
(b) A Joint Meet?
(c) 'By Invitation'?

586 What do the following have in common:
Ardingly, Honiton, Peterborough?

587 Name two of the aims of autumn hunting.

In the following questions select the answer closest in meaning.

588 A 'Babbler' is —
(a) A brook in hilly country?
(b) A hound which speaks when there is no scent?
(c) A noisy member of the field?
(d) A broken-winded horse?

589 To 'enter' hounds is —
    (*a*) To box them to take them to the meet?
    (b) To put them into covert?
    (*c*) To make the entries for a hound show?
    (*d*) To educate young hounds in the field?

590 'Owning a line' is —
    (*a*) Telling tall stories about feats in the hunting field?
    (*b*) When hounds speak with certainty?
    (*c*) Possessing several horses with the same breeding?
    (*d*) To own the land over which a hunted fox has run?

591 'Getting to the bottom of a horse' means —
    (*a*) Tiring it out?
    (*b*) Plaiting its tail?
    (*c*) Catching up the horse in front?
    (*d*) A fall off the back end?

592 A 'skirter' is —
    (*a*) An article of clothing worn when riding side-saddle?
    (*b*) A female follower of hounds?
    (*c*) A hound which does not hunt the true line?
    (*d*) A male follower who pays undue attention to the ladies in the hunting field?

593 'Coffee-housing' is —
    (*a*) Idle chatter at the covert side?
    (*b*) A car-followers' picnic?
    (*c*) A meeting of the Hunt Committee?
    (*d*) A fall into dirty water?

594 What is meant by 'larking over fences'? —
    (*a*) When your horse is jumping 'like a bird'?
    (*b*) Putting rails into wire to make a safe jump?
    (*c*) Jumping a succession of fences in a fast hunt?
    (*d*) Jumping fences unnecessarily, particularly when hounds are not running?

595 What is the 'Tally'? —
    (*a*) The number of hounds in kennel?
    (*b*) The number of followers at the end of a hunt?
    (*c*) The annual subscription to the hunt?
    (*d*) The number of foxes accounted for in a season?

596 What do you say to bid farewell when you finish hunting and go home?

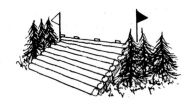

Horse Trials

597 The first three-day event ever held in England —
(a) Was a direct consequence of which Olympic Games?
(b) Was held in what year?
(c) Where?
(d) Who was the host?
(e) Who won?

598 Where was the first one-day horse trial held in England?

599 To which phase of the three-day event is a multiplying factor applied?

600 What is included in the speed and endurance phases of a three-day event?

601 What is the maximum height allowed for cross-country fences in Pony Club horse trials?

602 What is the minimum height of horse which may be registered for BHS horse trials?

603 What is the 'Box'?

604 Who introduced interval training to horse trials?

605 Which horse trials first introduced the following fences —
(a) Coffin?
(b) Normandy Bank?
(c) Rails arranged in a series of 'steps' along a slope?

606 At which horse trials would you find the following features —
(a) Queen Mary's Bower?
(b) Capability's Cutting?
(c) Bourne Crossing?
(d) Vicarage Ditch?

607 In which Olympic Games did Great Britain first win a three-day event gold medal?

608 In which Olympic Games did a British rider first win an individual gold medal? Who were rider and horse?

609 To whom is the Calcutta Light Horse Challenge Cup awarded?

610 Who first won Badminton, or its equivalent at Windsor in 1955 —
(a) Twice?
(b) Three times?
(c) Four times?
(d) Five times?
(e) Six times?

611 Which horse went under a fence and not over it, without penalty, and who was the rider?

612 Who were the husband and wife who rode for different countries at the same World Three-Day Event Championships? For which countries did they ride?

Dressage

613 What is the size of the small dressage arena?

614 What is the size of the large arena?

615 Name the arena letters in the correct order clockwise, starting at C.

616 By which letter does the rider enter the arena?

617 Which letter is in the centre of the arena?

618 Which extra letters are used when setting out a large arena?

619 Into how many categories or lists are official dressage judges grouped?

620 In 1957 The Dressage Grand Prix at Aachen Horse Show, at the time the most prestigious in Europe, was won by a British rider. Can you name both rider and horse?

621 Which British rider was bronze medallist in the World Dressage Championships held at Goodwood in 1978?

622 Which 17th-century English nobleman wrote a book, was a master of High School, and introduced dressage to England?

623 Which 18th-century French riding master is remembered as the first to describe shoulder-in and as the developer of many of the classical movements performed today?

Show Jumping

624 What does BSJA stand for?

625 When was the BSJA founded?

626 What are the three grades into which horses are placed for adult competition?

627 What are the grades for junior competitions?

628 What is the maximum height of a pony in affiliated competitions?

629 What is the maximum age for Juniors?

630 When and how can junior members compete against adults?

631 What is the normal distance for ponies between two upright elements of a combination fence, for —
(a) One non-jumping stride?
(b) Two non-jumping strides?

632 What is the related distance between two fences four strides apart?

633 Why do course-builders use shorter distances when building indoors?

634 Which BSJA table is used to judge competitions —
(a) When penalties are converted into seconds?
(b) When the course is divided into two sections?

635 What are the five different speeds at which competitions under Table A are judged?

636 What is the relation between time allowed and the time limit?

637 When is a water jump not a water jump?

638 In which competition is a practice fence included in the jump-off course?

639 Who bears overall responsibility for the course and the correct measurement of its distance?

640 What are the penalties for the following faults —
(a) Starting before the signal?
(b) Failing to start within 45 seconds of the signal?
(c) Disobedience at an obstacle for over 60 seconds?

641 At what stage is the clock stopped if a competitor refuses, and at the same time knocks down a pole and falls off?

642 When and where did show jumping begin?

643 Which major show is run by the BSJA?

644 Where is the British Jumping Derby held?

645 Which British rider was the first to win three British Jumping Derbys?

646 At which shows are the following competed for —
(a) The King George V Cup?
(b) The Cock o' the North Championship?
(c) The Aga Khan Trophy?

647 What is the ladies' equivalent of the King George V Cup?

648 Which Olympic Gold medal show jumper had his name given to a series of jumping competitions?

649 How many members make up a Nations Cup team, and how many rounds does each have to jump?

650 What trophy is awarded to the country gaining most points in a year in Nation Cups?

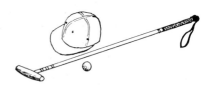

Polo

651 How many players make up a polo team?

652 What is the number of the team-member playing 'back'?

653 What are the periods of play called?

654 How many periods make a full match?

655 What is —
(a) The highest handicap given to the best players?
(b) The lowest handicap awarded?

656 Who has 'right of way' on the polo ground?

657 What constitutes 'off-side'?

658 What is the rule about left-handed players?

659 What are the three fixed distances from an opponent's goal from which penalties are taken?

660 What equipment is compulsory for ponies?

661 What is the size of an unboarded polo ground?

662 How wide is the goal?

663 What is the ruling body of English polo?

Driving

664 What are the four phases which can make up a driving event?

665 How are these four phases grouped into three 'Competitions'?

666 How many competitions must there be to make a Horse Driving Trials event?

667 What is judged under 'Presentation'?

668 Does the same vehicle have to be used throughout a driving trials?

669 Do the same horses and ponies have to be used throughout a driving trials?

670 What in driving is the dividing line between horses and ponies?

671 What terms describe —
(a) Two horses driven side by side?
(b) Two horses driven one in front of the other?
(c) Four horses driven to a vehicle?

672 Is there a weight limit for vehicles?

673 On how many different carriages may grooms and passengers ride over the marathon section?

674 Which of the driver, grooms, and passengers may handle —
(a) The reins?
(b) The whip?
(c) The brake?

675 What is the size of the dressage arena —
(a) For teams and tandems?
(b) For pairs and singles?

676 How do the letters around a driving dressage arena differ from those used in mounted dressage?

Long Distance Riding

677 What qualities are tested in Long Distance Riding?

678 Over how many days does the Golden Horseshoe Ride take place?

679 What distance must be covered on each day of the Golden Horseshoe Ride?

680 What distance must be covered in a qualifying ride?

681 At what speed must the course be covered to gain a gold award?

682 Who awards penalties?

683 What distance must be covered in the Goodwood International Ride. Over how many days?

684 How is the winner of the Goodwood Ride decided?

Showing

685 What does WHP stand for?

686 How do the height limits for WHP differ from those for ridden pony classes?

687 In a WHP class —
(a) How is the judging divided into two parts?
(b) What changes, if any, may be made in rider and tack between the two parts?

688 What dress is correct for the rider in a ridden pony class?

689 In leading rein classes —
(a) What are the height limits?
(b) Where should the leading rein be attached?
(c) What bit may be used?

690 At what paces are first-ridden ponies required to go?

691 Which breeds are included in mountain and moorland classes?

692 Welsh ponies are divided into sections —
(a) What are the sections called?
(b) In which section would a 14.2 hand Welsh cob be placed?

693 In which ridden classes are competitors not required to gallop all together as a class?

694 Which categories of horses are shown in hand?

695 What are the five different ridden classes for show hunters?

696 For which ridden hunter and hack classes would a 14.3 hand horse be eligible by height?

Racing

697 What is the governing body for racing in the United Kingdom?

698 What did cross-country races with a church steeple as the winning post become known as?

699 What are amateur race meetings held by hunts known as?

700 What is the earliest age at which thoroughbred horses race?

701 Name the five English classic races.

702 Over what distance is the Derby run?

703 Which classic race is run on Town Moor?

704 What is the greatest number of classic races won by one horse?

705 Which jockey holds the record for riding the greatest number of classic winners?

706 When this record was made in 1984, the previous record had stood for —
(a) 34 years?
(b) 68 years?
(c) 123 years?
(d) 157 years?

707 What makes the Grand National fences different from those on other courses?

708 What are the three different types of fence used to make up a steeplechase course?

709 Name four of the winning margins used to describe the result of a race.

710 Which horse —
(a) Won the Grand National three times?
(b) Was know as 'the spotted wonder'?
(c) Was '...first, the rest nowhere'?
(d) Won the Derby and the Irish Derby and was kidnapped at stud?

711 On which courses are the following races run —
(a) The Grand National?
(b) The Derby?
(c) The Eclipse Stakes?
(d) The King George VI and Queen Elizabeth Stakes?
(e) The King George VI Steeplechase?
(f) The Town Plate?

712 With which racecourses do you associate —
  (*a*) The Bushes?
  (*b*) Becher's Brook?
  (*c*) Tattenham Corner?
  (*d*) The Railway Fences?
  (*e*) The Limekilns?
  (*f*) The Roodee?
  (*g*) Swinley Bottom?
  (*h*) The Knavesmire?
  (*i*) The Melling Road?

713 With which famous jockeys do you connect —
  (*a*) The Tinman?
  (*b*) 'Come on Steve'?
  (*c*) The Head Waiter?
  (*d*) The Shoe?
  (*e*) The Longfellow?

714 What in racing terms is —
  (*a*) A Plate?
  (*b*) The post?
  (*c*) Stalls?
  (*d*) A Ringer?
  (*e*) The Ring?
  (*f*) The Tapes?
  (*g*) Silks?
  (*h*) A Walkover?

715 For which 'Firsts' are the following known —
  (*a*) Meriel Tufnell?
  (*b*) Jenny Pitman?
  (*c*) Diana Thorne?
  (*d*) Geraldine Rees?
  (*e*) Lorna Vincent?

716 Why in 1983 were the first five horses in the Cheltenham Gold Cup all paraded in the winners enclosure?

717 Which two races make up —
  (*a*) The Spring Double?
  (*b*) The Autumn Double?

718 What is —
  (*a*) A racecard?
  (*b*) The paddock?
  (*c*) A bumper?
  (*d*) A permit holder?

719 When is a horse —
    (*a*) Upsides?
    (*b*) Half-lengthed?

720 What position in the result of a race is 'also ran'?

721 Which Queen laid out Ascot racecourse?

722 Who was the first professional jockey to be knighted, who was also champion jockey 26 times?

723 Who was champion National Hunt jockey four times, leading National Hunt trainer seven times and has ridden and trained the winner of every important National Hunt race?

724 Who, as the 'Master of Ballydoyle', trained four Cheltenham Gold Cup winners, three Champion Hurdle winners and three successive Grand National winners?

725 What is the colour of the flag hoisted at the end of a race to indicate 'all right'?

SOME GENERAL QUESTIONS

The 'Equine Connection'

There is a connection, through horses and ponies, between all the items listed in each question — Can you see what it is?

726 Yew, laburnum, ragwort, hemlock, deadly nightshade?

727 Stripe, snip, star, blaze?

728 Wheelbarrow, shovel, skep, broom?

729 Pincers, rasp, hammer, anvil?

730 Webbing, Balding, threefold, nylon?

731 Safety pin, scissors, Stockholm tar, surgical tape?

732 Lice, sweet-itch, ringworm, warbles?

733 Holstein, Hanoverian, Oldenburg, Mecklenburg?

734 Gullet, waist, skirt, seat?

735 Ruby, Ranter, Royal, Bellman?

736 Rubber, vulcanite, wood, leather, stainless steel?

737 Cecil Smith, Harry Highover, Dick Christian, Dr Bristol?

738 Levade, courbette, capriole, ballotade, croupade?

739 Park Drag, Barouche, Victoria, Brougham?

740 Carrots, mangolds, swedes, turnips?

741 Milk, eggs, beer, oatmeal?

742 Dogstail, Timothy, Fescue, Cocksfoot?

743 Leather, felt, sorbo-rubber, sponge, sheepskin, nylon?

744 Quartering, strapping, brush-over, set-fair?

745 Bog, bone, occult?

746 Brigham, Buckskin Joe, Old Charlie, Tall Bull?

747 Salisbury, Cheltenham, Wellington, Rugby?

748 Kentucky Derby, Preakness Stakes, Belmont Stakes?

749 Greatwood, Tarwood, Waterloo, Billesdon Coplow?

750 Jericho Gorse, Christmas Gorse, Sheepthorns, Aunt Mary's Bottom?

751 Conversano, Maetoso, Neapolitano, Pluto, Siglavy, Favory?

752 Face, step, table, throat?

753 Patten, rocker-bar, anchor, three-quarter bar?

754 Godolphin Arabian, Darley Arabian, Byerley Turk?

755 Head, neck, shank, point?

Over the Seas and Far Away

Questions on horses from all parts of the world.

756 Which continent has given its name to a horse sickness?

757 Where is the Blue Grass Country?

758 In which country would you find the Spanish Riding School?

759 Where is Punchestown, famous for its racecourse and horse trials?

760 By what two names are American cow ponies known?

761 What is an Australian wild horse?

762 What are those French riding instructors who wear a black uniform called?

763 In which countries do the following important events take place —
(*a*) The Calgary Stampede?
(*b*) Maryland Hunt Cup?
(*c*) Durban July Handicap?
(*d*) Pardubice Steeplechase?
(*e*) Keeneland Sales?
(*f*) Melbourne Cup?
(*g*) Prix de l'Arc de Triomphe?

764 What breed was founded in 1789 when an American horse called 'Justin Morgan' was foaled?

765 In which Italian city is an annual horse race, called the Palio, held around the main square?

766 What is the English equivalent of colours known in America as —
(a) Sorrel?
(b) Pinto?

767 Where would you find the 'wild white horses of the sea'?

768 What name is given to the American horse which is bred to race over quarter of a mile?

769 How was the mail taken from Missouri to San Francisco in 1860?

770 Which horse trials fence is named after a Prussian breed?

771 For what was the Kadir Cup awarded?

772 In which country was the Falabella or miniature horse first bred?

773 What did Professor Przevalski discover in 1881?

774 Which country included three members of the same family in its national three-day event team at the same time? Who were they?

775 What is the American term for riding a flat race with the outside stirrup leather shorter than the inside?

Take Your Pick

In this section each word has been given four possible alternative interpretations. Select the one which you think is closest to the correct meaning.

776 Gamgee —
(a) Cotton wool encased in gauze.
(b) A jelly to apply to wounds.
(c) A webbing girth.
(d) Radiation treatment.

777 Gall —
(a) A French breed of pony.
(b) A head collar.
(c) A sore place.
(d) A feed additive.

778 Sweet Itch —
    (a) The consequence of overfeeding sugar beet.
    (b) Irritation of the mane and tail.
    (c) Lice.
    (d) A rough unhealthy coat.

779 Pritchel —
    (a) A two year old male deer.
    (b) A foot injury caused by a badly driven nail.
    (c) A farrier's tool.
    (d) A disease of the foot.

780 Overfaced —
    (a) A pony with a large head.
    (b) A pony discouraged by a big jump.
    (c) A pony with a lot of white on its face.
    (d) A pony which has been overtrained.

781 Over-reach —
    (a) A fall while trying to jump too wide a ditch.
    (b) A rug which covers the neck as well as the body.
    (c) Striking the inside of the knee with the opposite foot.
    (d) Striking the heel of a forefoot with the hind shoe.

782 Horse-sick —
    (a) Horse vomit.
    (b) Horse 'flu'.
    (c) Sour pasture.
    (d) A stable virus.

783 'Putting in a quick one' —
    (a) Cheating at mounted games.
    (b) Having a stiff drink before jumping a big track.
    (c) Changing legs when approaching a fence.
    (d) Putting in an extra stride at take off.

784 Roarer —
    (a) A Field Master with a loud voice.
    (b) A horse which 'makes a noise'.
    (c) A horse which goes up on his hind legs.
    (d) A dangerous horse.

785 Quittor —
    (a) An American bull whip.
    (b) A lazy racehorse.
    (c) A suppurating sore on the coronet.
    (d) An Indian hill pony.

786 Ratcatcher —
    (a) A hound better suited to ratting than hunting foxes.
    (b) Informal hunting dress.

(c) The terrierman.

(d) The stable cat.

787 Sulky —

(a) A sullen horse.

(b) A soft pad used to protect a sore back.

(c) A two-wheeled cart.

(d) The soft underhair of the winter coat.

788 Throat Latch —

(a) An obstruction in the windpipe.

(b) A strap used to discourage wind-sucking.

(c) A patent stable door fastener.

(d) Another name for throat lash.

789 Quiddor —

(a) A successful gambler at the races.

(b) A horse dealer.

(c) A groom employed at a livery stable.

(d) A horse which drops impacted lumps of food from his mouth.

790 Haflinger —

(a) A cross-over noseband.

(b) A trotting horse.

(c) An Austrian breed.

(d) A picture by 'Haflinger'.

791 Lampas —

(a) A material for making girths.

(b) A safety lamp for use in stables.

(c) A dressing for a bruised sole.

(d) A swelling on the roof of the mouth.

792 Hobday —

(a) A 19th-century equestrian author.

(b) A cross between a horse and a mule.

(c) An extra hunting day not advertised.

(d) An operation on the larynx.

793 'Going out of the front door' —

(a) When a horse escapes from his stable.

(b) A fall over your pony's head.

(c) Said of someone with a groom to bring the horse to the door.

(d) Leaving the ring without completing the course.

794 Roughing off —

(a) Gradual preparation for turning out to grass.

(b) Rasping the feet during shoeing.

(c) Rasping sharp edges off the teeth.

(d) A cruel method of breaking young horses.

795 Troika —
   (*a*) A Russian carriage.
   (*b*) Three horses driven abreast.
   (*c*) A High School movement.
   (*d*) Winner of the Triple Crown.

796 Counter Canter —
   (*a*) A true canter.
   (*b*) An exercise to engage the hocks.
   (*c*) When the horse leads with the outside foreleg.
   (*d*) A canter in four time.

797 Contact —
   (*a*) When a horse hits a pole without dislodging it.
   (*b*) The weight that you feel when you take up the reins.
   (*c*) The parts of the rider next to the horse.
   (*d*) The use of the lower leg to apply the aids.

798 Bascule —
   (*a*) The shape of the horse clearing a jump.
   (*b*) A French breed of saddle horse.
   (*c*) The phase before beginning High School work.
   (*d*) A patch of light hair on the quarters.

799 Acceptance of the bit —
   (*a*) The horse accepts the contact of the rider's hands on the reins.
   (*b*) The first state in mouthing a young horse.
   (*c*) The horse plays with the bit.
   (*d*) Another term for putting on the bridle.

800 Lateral Work —
   (*a*) Movements along the short side of a dressage arena.
   (*b*) Movement in a straight line with the fore and hind feet making different tracks.
   (*c*) Use of long reins to make the young horse flexible.
   (*d*) Moving from one side of a manège to the other.

801 Horse-Standard —
   (*a*) A measuring stick.
   (*b*) An American breed.
   (*c*) The set number of faults which if exceeded require that a show jumper retire.
   (*d*) The conditions for inclusion in a stud book.

802 Keratoma —
   (*a*) A Russian breed.
   (*b*) A wooden mouthpiece on a breaking bit.
   (*c*) A horny tumour in the foot.
   (*d*) A narrow leather strap.

803 Terret —
    (a) A ring through which driving reins pass.
    (b) A four wheeled driving vehicle.
    (c) A hay-loft.
    (d) A stimulant given to an exhausted horse.

804 Shadbelly —
    (a) A cut-away hunting coat.
    (b) A herring gutted horse.
    (c) A timid rider.
    (d) A leather harness belly band.

805 'Shooting your Wheelers' —
    (a) A wheelwright's term for putting new wheels on old axles.
    (b) A driving term for making the wheelers take the strain.
    (c) Washing down a carriage.
    (d) The unhappy consequence of a bad driving accident.

806 Waler —
    (a) A horse from South Wales.
    (b) A horse from New South Wales.
    (c) A horse used to beach whaling boats.
    (d) A whip made of whale bone.

807 Mitbah —
    (a) The produce of an Arab stallion and a donkey.
    (b) A Turkish pack saddle.
    (c) A breed of pony found in the marshlands of Iraq.
    (d) A term describing the angle at which the neck of an Arab horse joins the head.

808 Prophet's Thumb Mark —
    (a) A brand put on pure Arab horses.
    (b) A racing tip.
    (c) Dark patches of hair.
    (d) An indentation in the neck.

809 Transitions —
    (a) Changes of direction.
    (b) Changes of pace and speed.
    (c) Flying changes.
    (d) Jumping upright and spread fences alternately.

810 Jardon —
    (a) A boot worn by ponies pulling mowing machines.
    (b) A French carriage.
    (c) A tumour on the hock.
    (d) A disease of the foot.

A Visit to the Zoo?

If the conformation of a horse or pony is unusual, or faulty, it is often compared to other animals. For instance a horse with a prominent spine may be called 'hog-backed'.

The answer to each question in this section is the name of an animal, bird or fish — even a flower — used to describe different parts of the horse, his action and his colouring. Give the names of —

811 An 'upside down' neck, concave at the crest.

812 Quarters which slope sharply from the highest point to the root of the tail.

813 A horse with a belly line which slopes up sharply from the girth to the stifle.

814 Hocks which turn inwards at the points.

815 A very high head carriage, with a neck bulging out at the gullet.

816 A mouth where the teeth of the upper jaw overhang the lower.

817 A grey horse which has flecks of darker hairs in the coat.

818 A narrow upright hoof.

819 Turned-in toes.

820 A small mean eye.

821 Back at the knee.

822 A spine particularly high at the loins.

823 Long untidy hairs which appear in the coat after clipping.

824 A short, thick neck.

825 A long neck concave at the lower end.

826 A flashy appearance with a high head carriage.

827 The rudimentary teeth which appear in front of the molars.

828 Small dark marks on white hair around the coronet.

829 Stripes on the limbs, neck and quarters.

830 A tail with little or no hair on the dock.

831 A wide, loose, overhanging upper lip.

832 Flattish feet marked with ridges.

833 Dark spots on a lighter coloured coat.

834 A certain amount of white hair on the quarters.

835 A tail with the dock concave rather than convex.

836 A head with a convex profile.

837 A prominent eye.

838 A horse which doesn't seem to try, especially in racing.

839 A horse with a walk or trot action very close to the ground.

840 A horse inclined to spook.

Odd One Out

Find the connection and then spot the 'Odd One Out' in each of the following questions.

841 (a) Running (b) Standing (c) Irish (d) Grakle.

842 (a) Dartmoor (b) New Forest (c) Appaloosa (d) Fell.

843 (a) Brushing (b) Butcher (c) Hock (d) Over-reach.

844 (a) Hunter (b) Hogged (c) Blanket (d) Trace.

845 (a) Shredded paper (b) Peat (c) Shavings (d) Oat straw.

846 (a) Day (b) Night (c) Australia (d) New Zealand.

847 (a) Martingale (b) Girth (c) Surcingle (d) Breastplate.

848 (a) Body (b) Water (c) Curry (d) Dandy.

849 (a) Legs (b) Voice (c) Whip (d) Seat.

850 (a) Head (b) Tail (c) Stable (d) Exercise.

851 (a) Girth gall (b) Capped elbow (c) Sore back (d) Fistulous wither.

852 (a) Wind sucking (b) Weaving (c) Napping (d) Crib-biting.

853 (a) Andalusian (b) Breton (c) Camargue (d) Percheron.

854 (a) Thoroughpin (b) Windgall (c) Spavin (d) Curb.

855 (a) Shoulder (b) Elbow (c) Wrist (d) Hip.

856 (a) Colic (b) Thrush (c) Canker (d) Corn.

857 (a) Post and rails (b) Hedge (c) Taut wire (d) Chestnut paling.

858 (*a*) Calkin (*b*) Clench (*c*) Cradle (*d*) Clip.

859 (*a*) Polo (*b*) Gymkhana (*c*) Travelling (*d*) Sausage.

860 (*a*) Hay (*b*) Lucerne (*c*) Carrots (*d*) Apples.

861 (*a*) Gilpin (*b*) Herring (*c*) Aldin (*d*) Surtees.

862 (*a*) Ascot (*b*) Cheltenham (*c*) Newbury (*d*) Sandown.

863 (*a*) Warranty (*b*) Knocked-up (*c*) Knocked-down (*d*) Feather edge.

864 (*a*) Set Fast (*b*) Azoturia (*c*) Haemoglobinuria (*d*) Strangles.

865 (*a*) Ring (*b*) Round (*c*) Red (*d*) Whip.

Double Meanings

When you use one of the words in this section it could mean up to five different things — all of them something to do with horses or ponies. See if you can find at least two horsey meanings for each word below.

866 Chestnut.

867 Muzzle.

868 Curb.

869 Brush.

870 Cast.

871 Cheek.

872 Run-up.

873 Pull.

874 Bone.

875 Stud.

876 Whip.

877 Neck.

878 Going.

879 Forge.

880 Strap.

881 Clip.

882 Back.

883 Turn-out.

884 Girth.

885 Plait.

886 Bar.

887 Tread.

888 Cap.

889 Jockey.

890 Gullet.

891 Corn.

892 Horn.

893 Bolt.

894 Break.

895 Paddock.

896 Ribbons.

897 Acceptance.

898 Feather.

899 Boot.

900 Beans.

Books, Poems and Pictures

Some questions on the horse in literature and art.

901 Who said 'A horse, a horse, my Kingdom for a horse'?

902 Where was a fine lady seen on a white horse?

903 What couldn't 'all the King's horses' do?

904 Who set out to ride to the Bell at Edmonton on his wedding day?

905 Who wrote 'The best of my fun I owe it to horse and hound'?

906 Who rode from Boston to Lexington to warn of the approach of British troops?

907 Name two of the riders who rode to bring the good news from Ghent to Aix?

908 What was a mythological half man, half horse called?

909 Who were the riders of the following flying horses—
(a) Pegasus?
(b) Al Borak?
(c) Shadowfax?

910 Who owned the horses —
(a) Lamri?
(b) Bridgadore?

911 What was the name of the horse of the four sons of Aymon which grew large or smaller according to which son rode it?

912 What was the name of the great white war horse of the Spanish hero El Cid?

913 What colour was the horse of 'Faithful and True'?

914 Which Roman Emperor made his horse a consul and what was the horse called?

915 Who owned Bucephalus?

916 How did Darius' horse gain him the throne of Persia?

917 Name the horse of highwayman Tom Faggus in Lorna Doone.

918 In what sport did the Maltese Cat excel?

919 Which horse did Charles Cothill ride in the English Chaser's Cup round Compton Course?

920 What was the name of the favourite for the Wessex Cup tracked down by Sherlock Holmes?

921 Where did hounds meet on the day of the Ghost Heath run?

922 What was the name of the horse which Vronsky rode in the Great Steeplechase?

923 In which series of stories would you meet Major Yeates and Flurry Knox?

924 What happened to Jack's pony Tom?

925 Who wrote —
(a) National Velvet?
(b) The Red Pony?
(c) My Friend Flicka?
(d) The Nutcrackers and the Sugartongs?
(e) No Mistaking Corker?
(f) The Young Horse-Breakers?

926 In which poem do the following riders and ponies all appear — Diana, Prunella on Guzzle, Monica, Joan on Smudges?

927 What was the title of the first book written by Dick Francis?

928 Identify the following characters in books by R.S. Surtees —
(a) The City grocer from Great Coram Street.
(b) The MFH of the Flat Hat Hunt
(c) His double and inseparable companion.
(d) Known as 'Soapey'.
(e) Known as 'Facey'.
(f) Old Jog.
(g) The huntsman from 'Cannynewcassel'.
(h) The odd-job boy and whip who liked marmalade.

929 In which poem did 'Hard riding Dick spend his youth in the stable without any wage'?

930 Complete the following —
(a) You can take a horse to water but you cannot . . . .
(b) Straight from the horse's . . . .
(c) As strong as a . . . .
(d) Don't look a gift horse . . . .
(e) 'Tis a good horse that never . . . .
(f) Boot, saddle . . . . and away.

931 Fill in the missing line —
'Before the Gods that made the Gods
Had seen their sunrise pass

. . . .
Was cut out of the grass.'

932 Complete the following —
'For want of a nail, the shoe was lost;
For want of a shoe, ... ?

933 Who 'rode their horses up to bed'?

934 Gulliver's last voyage took him to a land of horses. What were the horses and their human slaves called?

935 What was Don Quixote's horse called?

936 Who was known as 'Mr . . . . the horse painter'?

937 Which French artist suffered a crippling riding accident as a child yet still painted horse pictures?

938 From which ancient civilization has a statuette survived of a flying horse standing on a swallow?

939 Which French artist painted and sculpted horses and ballet dancers?

940 Which artist published 'The Anatomy of the Horse'?

941 Who painted 'Scotland forever — The Charge of the Scots Greys at Waterloo'?

942 Who started life as a stage coachman and painted eighteen Derby winners?

943 Who painted 'Horse Frightened by Lightning'?

944 Who painted 'After the Race — Cheltenham Saddling Paddock'?

945 Who painted 'The Finest View in Europe'?

The Numbers Game

How Many —

946 Inches in 16 hands?

947 Foxes in a brace?

948 Foxes in a leash?

949 Nails in a horse shoe?

950 Rings on a Scorrier snaffle?

951 False ribs in a horse?

952 True ribs in a horse?

953 Molars in a mature horse's mouth?

954 Cheltenham Gold Cups were won by Golden Miller?

955 Queen Alexandra Stakes were won by Brown Jack?

956 Times was Eclipse beaten on the racecourse?

957 Horsemen of the Apocalypse?

958 Legendary Chinese Emperor's horses?

959 Bronze horses on St Mark's Venice?

960 Rode Tom Pearce's grey mare?

The End of the Road

Including all those questions which haven't fitted in anywhere else —

961 What do the following initials stand for —
(a) RDA?
(b) FEI?
(c) CCIO?
(d) CDIO?
(e) CSIO?

962 What is a mare used for breeding called?

963 When and where does Galvayne's groove appear?

964 What is 'Bishoping'?

965 From which grey horse are all grey Thoroughbreds descended?

966 In which year were the first equestrian events in the Modern Olympiad held?

967 How much saliva does a horse make make every 24 hours —
(a) 6 pints?
(b) 6 litres?
(c) 6 quarts?
(d) 6 gallons?

968 What percentage of water makes up the bodyweight of a foal —
(a) 25%
(b) 50%
(c) 60%
(d) 80%

969 In which stages of The Duke of Edinburgh's Award are mounted expeditions included?

970 What Pony Club efficiency certificates are required for each of these stages?

971 Which breed of heavy horse has no feathers and is always chestnut?

972 When and where was the first Midnight Steeplechase held?

973 What is a 'Rosinback'?

974 When you are working with other horses in a riding school, on which side should you pass?

975 Smallness can be greatness. How high were —

    (*a*) Hyperion, Derby and St Leger winner and influential sire?

    (*b*) Stroller, Olympic silver medal individual show jumper?

976 What name is given to a trotting gait in which the near fore and near hind move together?

977 Where would you find a 'Fireman' with a 'Doorman'?

978 What great equestrian feat was performed by A.F.Tschiffely and his horses Mancho and Gato?

979 Each of the following horses had a name starting with 'Black' —

    (*a*) Dick Turpin's horse.

    (*b*) The title of a book by Anna Sewell.

    (*c*) The Earl of Warwick's horse.

    (*d*) One of Mary Queen of Scots' horses.

    (*e*) The sire from whom all Tennessee Walking Horses are descended.

980 Who is the Patron Saint of Horsemen?

SOME LOCAL QUESTIONS FOR QUIZ MASTERS

981 What is the full and correct name of your Pony Club Branch?

982 Who is your DC?

983 Who is the Branch Secretary?

984 Name two other members of the Branch Committee.

985 Who is Branch Chief Instructor?

986 In which Area is your Branch?

987 Who is the Area Representative?

988 Name four other Branches in the Area.

989 Who is the Chairman of the Pony Club?

990 Which Inter-Branch competitions did your Branch enter this/last year?

991 Name one team member in each Inter-Branch team.

992 Name one landowner or farmer who has hosted a rally.

993 Name one instructor who has taught you at a rally.

994 When was your Branch founded?

995 Where was the last Branch camp held?

996 Name one local show or event, not run by the Pony Club, which stages a competition for Pony Club members.

997 Which Hunt hunts your Branch area?

998 What is the name of the MFH/MH?

999 What efficiency standard have you passed? What is the next standard you can take? How soon can you take it?

1000 What events other than rallies has the Branch held in the last year?

ANSWERS

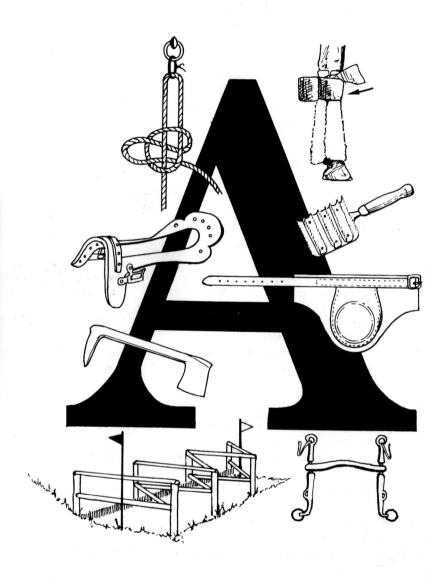

EQUITATION

1 *Girths secure; stirrup irons down; stirrup leathers approximately the correct length; saddle flaps lying smoothly.*

2 *No. You should be able to mount from either side.*

3 *Measure against your arm from knuckles to armpit.*

4 *Stand in front and compare them by eye.*

5 *With your left shoulder by the pony's near shoulder.*

6 *Left hand.*

7 *They must be short enough to prevent the pony from moving off. If you are mounting from the near-side, the off-side rein should be slightly shorter than the near-side.*

8 *Helping someone to mount by giving a lift to the left leg (if mounting from the near-side).*

9 *Use a mounting block. Get a leg-up. Lengthen the stirrup-leather until you can reach the stirrup (shorten it when mounted).*

10 *On your right side.*

11 *(a) Keep both feet in the stirrups (b) Hold the reins in the hand opposite to the stirrup being adjusted (c) Hold it in the same hand as the reins.*

12 *Between third and fourth fingers, then between first finger and thumb.*

13 *Straight line from bit through the reins and hands to the elbow.*

14 *Legs, hands, seat (and body); voice.*

15 *Whip, spurs.*

16 *(a) The lowest part (b) The ball of the foot (c) Enough to keep the iron in place.*

17 *Your hands move in harmony with the pony's head.*

18 *No. You should be able to dismount on either side.*

19 *(a) Remove them from the stirrups. (b) Place them in the left hand if dismounting on the near-side. (c) In the same hand as the reins.*

20 *To soothe, scold, or as an aid to training the young pony.*

21 *The standard of the rider and the type of work being done.*

22 *When you have an independent seat and complete control of your legs.*

23 *When your seat returns to the saddle as the off-hind and near-fore legs come to the ground.*

24 *Sit in the saddle for an extra beat.*

25 *When changing direction, and at frequent intervals while hacking.*

26 *Left diagonal on the right rein, right diagonal on the left rein.*

27 *The weight should not vary.*

28 *(b)*

29 *In the direction in which he is going.*

30 *The inside hand.*

31 *(a) 4 (b) 2 (c) 3 (d) 4.*

32 *Near hind, near fore, off hind, off fore.*

33 *The trot.*

34 *A nudge behind the girth.*

35 *To reinforce the leg aid.*

36 *Forward over the knees and stirrups.*

37 *You will appear to sit on top of rather than into the saddle, or you will sit too far back.*

38 *You may fall behind the movement, lose your stirrups, or grip upwards,*

39 *You should shorten your stirrups.*

40 *A neck strap.*

41 *(a) Approach (b) Take-off (c) Moment of suspension (d) Landing (e) Get-away (recovery).*

42 *The approach.*

43 *Because it encourages the rider to lean and balance on the horse's neck.*

44 *Three.*

45 *Shortens the neck and raises the head.*

46 *They roll rather than fall down easily, and can cause unnecessary accidents.*

47 *When the base of a fence is set beyond the vertical.*

48 *A combination of two fences.*

49 *Lower the fence.*

50 *(a) Pain (b) Fear (c) Disobedience (d) Fatigue.*

51 *Overfacing.*

52 *They are the wrong distance for the walk stride.*

53 *Because the horse will be encouraged to jump them together. Use at least three.*

54 *To encourage the horse to relax, to keep a regular rhythm and to swing his back.*

55 *Midway between the poles.*

56 *The walk.*

57 *1.3 to 1.5 metres (4½ to 5 feet).*

58 *(a) Solid poles (b) Well filled and not airy (c) True ground line.*

59 *(a) Staircase or ascending oxer (b) Pyramid (c) Upright or vertical (d) True parallel or square oxer.*

60 *A bounce fence.*

61 *One.*

62 *They encourage the horse to jump the centre of the fence and help him to jump straight.*

63 *(a) The rider has greater control at the slower pace. (b) It is easier to be in the right place for 'take-off' (the trot stride is half the canter stride). (c) The horse has more time to size up the fence and less reason to be frightened.*

64 *Collected. Medium. Extended. Free.*

65 *On the same line as the outside fore-foot.*

66 *The inside leg with a quick nudge at the right moment.*

67 *(a) Outside (b) Outside (c) Inside.*

68 *Almost in two-time.*

69 *Near-hind and off-fore together, off-hind and near-fore together.*

70 *In rein-back the hands do not allow forward movement.*

71 *Repeat the aid and use the whip.*

72 *'Running'.*

73 *(a) Irregular steps (b) Running (c) Loss of balance on to the forehand.*

74 *Collected. Working. Medium. Extended.*

75 *Near-hind, off-hind and near-fore together, off-fore.*

76 *When the leading hind leg appears to be on the opposite side to the leading fore leg.*

77 *The rider will bump in the saddle.*

78 *(a) Loss of balance on to the forehand (b) Quickening the tempo.*

79 *When no foot is on the ground.*

80 *Trot, canter, gallop. Also when jumping.*

81 *Evenly on all four legs.*

82 *(a),(c),(d),(e) are correct. (b),(f) are incorrect.*

83 *Impulsion.*

84 *Rhythm.*

85 *180°.*

86 *Walk and canter.*

87 *Maintains the impulsion and ensures that rhythm and tempo remain the same.*

88 *Working trot.*

89 *(c) and (d).*

90 *In the early stages on three tracks and later sometimes on four tracks.*

91 *When the hind feet cover the tracks made by the fore feet.*

92 *(b) and (c).*

93 *They do not encourage forward movement, and the hindquarters are lightened rather than engaged.*

94 *(a) and (c) only.*

95 *30°.*

96 *(a)*

97 *Loss of freedom of the inside shoulder (cramped).*

98 *Working trot.*

99 *Develop (a) Balance (b) Rhythm (c) Timing (d) An eye for distance (e) Riding a correct track.*

100 *The horse may try to jump the bounce in one leap.*

HORSEMASTERSHIP AND STABLE MANAGEMENT

The Grass-kept Pony

101 *May to September.*

102 *In winter and, if in work, in summer.*

103 *At least once a day.*

104 *It causes laminitis.*

105 *Shade and the companionship of another pony to keep flies away.*

106 *His legs and lungs are in constant use.*

107 *Excessive grooming removes grease from the coat which gives protection against wet and cold.*

108 *He is less likely to catch a chill as he moves about rather than standing still in a stable.*

109 *Wind.*

110 *In summer to avoid the flies.*

111 *To trap flies.*

112 *When two ponies are together one cannot get cornered.*

113 *By day in winter; by night in summer.*

114 *Post and rails.*

115 *0.3m (1 foot).*

116 *One acre.*

117 *New Zealand.*

Handling and Leading

118 *With your voice.*

119 *His shoulder.*

120 *Pat his lower neck or shoulder.*

121 *Leather or nylon.*

122 *Webbing or rope.*

123 *The back 'D'.*

124 *Towards the tail.*

125 *The toe.*

126 *Level with his shoulders.*

127 *One hand near the headcollar, the other at or near the free end.*

128 *A snaffle bridle.*

129 *Away from you.*

130 *No. From either side.*

131 *(a) With the reins straight to your hand.*
(b) With the far rein through the nearest snaffle ring.
(c) With a coupling linking the snaffle rings and a rope attached to the coupling.
(d) With a leading rein attached to the nearest ring and to the cavesson noseband next to this ring.

132 *Beside your knee.*

133 *(a) Around the neck.*
(b) If long enough, put the reins under the stirrup irons.

134 *Detach it from the reins and secure it to the neckstrap.*

135 *Showing off a pony by leading him on foot without a rider.*

136 *Stand in front, facing the pony, and hold the bit or headcollar with one hand on either side.*

137 *On your left side, putting yourself between the pony and the traffic.*

138 *Get an assistant to move him from behind or use a long whip in your outside hand behind your body.*

Stabling

139 *So that with the top half open the horse can look out and get fresh air.*

140 *Two: one at the top and one at the bottom.*

141 *To prevent the horse (a) Jumping out (b) Biting passers-by (c) Opening the top bolt (d) Weaving.*

142 *1.25m (4 feet).*

143 *Opening inwards it could jam against bedding or a cast horse.*

144 *(a) The horse cannot move around, and (b) cannot look out, so gets bored. (c) There is no direct access to fresh air. (d) Bullying may upset a shy or nervous horse.*

145 *It must be high enough to prevent a horse getting a leg over.*

146 *Non-slip; impervious to moisture; long wearing.*

147 *By a slightly sloping floor to a drain either outside the box, or in a corner away from manger, haynet and door.*

148 *Draughts.*

149 *A tying-up ring.*

150 *Manger, hayrack or hay-ring, water-bowl.*

151 *Level with the horse's chest.*

152 *Outside the stable, where the horse cannot interfere with it.*

153 *The log should just touch the ground when the pony stands up to the manger.*

154 *(a) To encourage the horse to lie down (b) To encourage him to stale (c) To provide insulation (d) To avoid jarring the feet.*

155 *Wheat.*

156 *When the horse is given a light brushover, droppings are removed and the bedding is tidied up.*

157 *The awns irritate the skin unless removed. It is palatable.*

158 *(a) Spray the straw with disinfectant; (b) Muzzle the horse; (c) Change to shavings or peat.*

159 *Every time you visit the stable.*

160 *When it is 0.3 m (1 foot) deep, say, every 3 to 4 months.*

161 *To short-rack or rack-up.*

162 *1.5m (5 feet).*

163 *Three heaps — the oldest ready for the garden, the next in process of rotting, the third for adding to.*

164 *Cover his head with a coat or wet sack before leading him out.*

165 *Inhaling smoke.*

Clothing

166 *Day rug, night rug and horse blankets.*

167 *(a) Anti-sweat rug (b) Waterproof rug (c) Summer sheet.*

168 *Roller.*

169 *Waterproof outer-covering with leg straps to keep the rug in place.*

170 *Fillet string.*

171 *To keep the legs warm and to prevent wet legs from becoming chapped.*

172 *10 cms (4 ins.)*

173 *(a) and (b).*

174 *Gamgee or softened straw.*

175 *A knot at front or back puts pressure on bone or tendon.*

176 *With a reef knot and by sewing both tape and bandage.*

177 *It will fall off or slip, unless it has been put on too tightly.*

178 *On the tail not the bandage.*

179 *Brushing, coronet, knee, hock, over-reach, polo, sausage, speedicut, tendon, travelling.*

Grooming

180 *Body-brush, dandy-brush, water-brush.*

181 *To clean the body-brush.*

182 *Stable rubber.*

183 *Wisp.*

184 *Body-brush.*

185 *Saddle region, head, points of hocks, fetlocks and pasterns.*

186 *Tap them to see if they are secure and run your fingers over the clenches.*

187 *Half to three-quarters of an hour.*

Clipping

188 *To (a) enable a horse to do fast work without distress (b) avoid heavy sweating (c) permit a horse to work longer, faster and better (d) dry off quickly (e) save labour (f) prevent disease.*

189 *Dry and clean.*

190 *The shoulder.*

191 *Head, groin and belly.*

192 *Inside the ears.*

193 *An all-over clip except for legs and saddle patch.*

194 *The hair is removed from the neck and belly, leaving a patch as though a blanket had been left on the body.*

195 *Trace. Belly and neck.*

196 *To protect against cold, mud and thorns.*

197 *Keep him warm with a rug and blankets.*

198 *When the new (winter) coat is well established or when the coat is too thick for the work being given.*

199 *Not later than the last week of January.*

200 *After exercise or on a warm day.*

201 *Remove the clipper head, clean, strip and oil.*

202 *Complete removal of the mane by clipping.*

203 *Six.*

204 *Sewing and rubber bands.*

205 *They 'pull' and are uncomfortable.*

206 *A bang-tail.*

207 *A switch-tail.*

208 *The coat is beginning to change.*

Feeding

209 *Oats.*

210 *It may hot-up some ponies.*

211 *1½ hours.*

212 *½ hour.*

213 *A horse or pony that does not thrive on normal quantities of feed.*

214 *A horse which needs coaxing to eat a normal feed.*

215 *Molasses or sugar beet pulp which has been soaked.*

216 *At least 4 to 6 hours.*

217 *A horse that throws his feed out of the manger.*

218 *(a) Keep a brick in the manger (b) Keep a lump of rocksalt in the manger (c) Fit bars across the manger (d) Use a noseband.*

219 *Sugar beet nuts or pulp.*

220 *Bran.*

221 *3 weeks.*

222 *The same food value. Barley is less likely to 'hot-up' a horse.*

223 *Round or square pieces can lodge in the throat.*

224 *6 months.*

225 *In heaps, one heap more than the number of ponies.*

226 *Seed and meadow hay.*

227 $^1/_{50}$.

228 *11.3 to 13.6 kg (25 to 30 lbs).*

229 *Three times.*

230 *Eye-level.*

231 *Chopped hay or straw used to provide bulk.*

232 *Twice a day.*

233 *By drinking from a shallow stream with a sandy bottom.*

The Foot and Shoeing

234 *(a) Sole (b) Frog (c) Bars.*

235 *The frog.*

236 *The coronet.*

237 *(a) A loose shoe (b) Worn shoes (c) Clenches risen (d) Foot too long (e) A lost shoe.*

238 *A remove.*

239 *Losing a shoe.*

240 *That part of the nail which penetrates the wall and is turned over.*

241 *One on fore, two on hind.*

242 *A tool used to cut the clenches when removing a shoe.*

243 *Hot shoeing and cold shoeing.*

244 *Hot shoeing, because the shoe can be made to fit exactly.*

245 *When a nail is driven too close to the sensitive part of the hoof.*

246 *When a nail penetrates the sensitive part of the foot.*

247 *When the toe is rasped away to fit the shoe.*

248 *Fine-nailing.*

249 *Fullering.*

250 *To prevent injury to the opposite leg — e.g. by brushing.*

251 *Grass tip.*

252 *Checked for splits and cracks, and rasped to keep an even surface on the ground.*

Health

253 (a) Alert and pricking to and fro (b) Glossy and lying flat
(c) Loose and supple (d) Eyes open and bright with
membranes under the lids and the nostrils salmon pink.

254 8 to 12.

255 38°C (100-101°F).

256 36 to 42 beats per minute.

Exercise

257 Exercise, which should be varied.

258 (a) To exercise as an alternative to riding.
(b) To settle a horse before mounting and riding.
(c) When superficial injury to the horse prevents riding.
(d) When the rider cannot ride through injury.

259 (a) Boots for all four legs (b) Lungeing cavesson
(c) Lungeing rein (d) Lungeing whip (e) Saddle or roller
(f) Side reins (g) Snaffle bridle.

260 Hard hat and gloves.

261 The voice, the lungeing rein and the whip.

262 In a rising tone.

263 Walk in a small circle or turn on the spot.

264 (a) Walk him towards a barrier. (b) Gradually reduce the
size of the circle.

265 By saddling up and riding regularly.

Competitions and Hunting

266 6-8 kph (4-5 mph).

267 9-10 kph (6 mph).

268 One mile.

269 The horse is liable to kick.

270 The horse is young and excitable.

271 None. It is your responsibility to avoid other horses.

272 *Warmed to about 21°C (70°F).*

273 *Whether he is warm and dry.*

274 *(a)Trot him up to check his soundness (b) Examine saddle and girth regions (c) Groom him thoroughly and be alert to bumps, etc (d) Lead him in hand to take off stiffness (e) Make sure he can lie down and rest.*

Breeds, Colours, Age and Height

275 *Connemara, Dale, Dartmoor, Exmoor, Fell, Highland, New Forest, Shetland and Welsh.*

276 *Thoroughbred.*

277 *Half-bred.*

278 *It must be in the Stud Register of the Breed Society.*

279 *(a), (b) and (e) are breeds. (c) and (d) are types.*

280 *Muzzle, tips of the ears, mane, tail, and extremities of the legs.*

281 *The brown has brown points, the bay has black.*

282 *List.*

283 *Light, dark, liver.*

284 *Strawberry, bay, blue.*

285 *Piebald.*

286 *Skewbald.*

287 *Iron-grey.*

288 *Star.*

289 *Stripe.*

290 *Snip.*

291 *Blaze.*

292 *Wall-eye.*

293 *By examining the front (incisor) teeth.*

294 *Milk teeth.*

295 *3 years.*

296 *6 years.*

297 *7 years.*

298 *8 years.*

299 1st January.

300 The withers.

301 Hands.

302 Inches.

303 Four.

304 The Joint Measurement Scheme.

305 Only officially appointed measurers.

306 (a) Smooth and level ground (b) The horse standing square
with the poll in line with the withers (c) A measuring stick
with a spirit level must be used.

307 Shoes must be removed when measuring for a height
certificate. 12mm (½ inch) is allowed for Pony Club
measuring.

308 (a) It is part of the correct description of the horse
(b) Indicates size of saddlery, clothing, etc, on sale at a
saddlers (c) Enables horses to be classified for shows.

309 (a) Foal (b) Yearling (c)Filly (d) Mare (e) Gelding.

310 Mule.

311 Jennet.

Conformation

312 Boxy.

313 50°.

314 Brushing.

315 Dishing.

316 Can affect respiration and possibly cause whistling.

317 Roman-nosed.

318 Bad temper.

319 (a) Bad temper (b) Wilful and obstinate.

320 Tied-in below the knee.

321 To one side at right angles to the back line of the hock.

Saddlery

322 *Tack.*

323 *(a) To distribute the rider's weight more evenly over the horse's back.*
(b) To put the rider in the correct position.

324 *From the pommel to the cantle.*

325 *Crupper.*

326 *An extra girth strap attached to the points of the tree.*

327 *A broken tree.*

328 *Faulty design, or it needs re-stuffing.*

329 *The tree.*

330 *(a) To protect the back (b) To help spread the pressure from a spring-tree saddle (c) Temporarily for an ill-fitted saddle.*

331 *Webbing, leather, nylon and lampwick.*

332 *Leather.*

333 *The front two or the first and third.*

334 *Place a piece of flannel or blanket soaked in neatsfoot oil between the folds.*

335 *Their whole foot can slip through the iron.*

336 *By using safety stirrups.*

337 *With the points turned down.*

338 *Stainless steel.*

339 *12mm (½ inch).*

340 *Ordinary leather, rawhide, buffalo hide.*

341 *That the holes are still level with each other.*

342 *From time to time have the leathers shortened at the buckle end.*

343 *Pony, Cob, Full-size.*

344 *Cheek-piece.*

345 *Browband.*

346 *With the full width of the hand between it and the side of the jawbone.*

347 *With two fingers between it and the front of the face.*

348 *(a) To hold the curbchain if it comes unhooked (b) To prevent the cheeks of a Banbury action bit from revolving (c) To prevent a horse catching hold of the cheeks of a bit.*

349 *Leather, rubber over leather, linen, nylon and webbing.*

350 *The bridoon rein is wider and longer.*

351 *The bit rein.*

352 *To keep the reins in place and to prevent them from going over the head.*

353 *The windpipe and the neck.*

354 *Snaffle, double bridle and pelham.*

355 *Measured in inches. From 4½ to 6 inches.*

356 *With any joint straight it should protrude about 0.5m (¼ inch) on either side of the mouth.*

357 *The tongue and bars.*

358 *(a) Lips and corners of the mouth (b) Bars of the mouth (c) Tongue (d) Roof of the mouth (e) Poll (f) Chin groove (g) Nose.*

359 *The poll and chin groove.*

360 *The roof of the mouth.*

361 *The tongue.*

362 *Allows comfortable room for the tongue under a bar mouthpiece.*

363 *Nose, poll and chin groove.*

364 *The snaffle only.*

365 *(a) When he tries to open his mouth wide; (b) When he crosses his jaw (c) When he draws his tongue back or tries to get it over the bit.*

366 *Four fingers.*

367 *The cavesson noseband and the girth.*

368 *(b), (c) and (d).*

369 *It will stain the breeches.*

370 *Cold or tepid.*

371 *Saddle horse.*

372 *It is too wet and diluted.*

373 *Dressed with neatsfoot or similar oil and wrapped in newspaper.*

374 *The stitching.*

375 *Roughness and wear, particularly at joints where the tongue or lips may get pinched.*

376 (a) *Dandy-brush for brushing saddle linings, numnahs and web girths.*
(b) *Stable rubber for drying metalwork and covering a clean saddle.*

'CALL THE VET'

377 *Good health (a), (d) and (e). Ill health (b), (c), (f) and (g).*

378 *Eight.*

379 *At least once a year.*

380 *Wolf teeth.*

381 *Worms.*

382 (a) *Animalintex poultice* (b) *Antiseptic* (c) *Bandages*
(d) *Cotton wool* (e) *Gamgee* (f) *Safety pins* (g) *Scissors*
(h) *Surgical tape* (i) *Wound dressing.*

383 (a) *Under the top of the lower jaw* (b) *The cheek artery above and behind the eye* (c) *On the inside of the foreleg by the knee.*

384 *The tips of the fingers.*

385 (a) *In cases of severe injury* (b) *If the temperature of the horse is 39°C (102°F) or higher* (c) *If the farrier cannot find the cause of lameness* (d) *If you are in any doubt about your horse's health.*

386 *Make sure that the horse is ready wearing a head collar, and have hot water, soap and towel at hand.*

387 *Tie up at eye level with a rope about 0.6m (2ft) long.*

388 *Soft non-heating food, particularly bran mashes.*

389 *Overheating hard foods: eg oats, barley, beans.*

390 *Use separate forage and equipment. Anyone looking after a sick horse, as well as a healthy one, must wear washable clothing, and change between tasks.*

391 *Every 4 hours.*

392 (a) *In the feed* (b) *In drinking water* (c) *On the tongue.*

393 *Wounds, so long as flies can be kept away; and lameness.*

394 *If bandaging or poulticing is needed, or if he has a temperature.*

395 *Several times a day.*

396 *By fitting a cradle.*

397 *Grease the heel thoroughly.*

398 *20 minutes.*

399 *In fomentation hot towels are applied; in hot tubbing the limb is immersed in water.*

400 *(a) To sooth bruising (b) To reduce inflammation (c) To clean wounds (d) To draw off pus.*

401 *(a) Clean cut (b) Tears (c) Punctures (d) Bruises (e) Galls.*

402 *(a) Stop bleeding (b) Clean up (c) Dress (d) Protect.*

403 *Use a pebble in a handkerchief tied above the wound so that it presses against the blood vessel.*

404 *Saddle and girth galls.*

405 *Girth itch.*

406 *Sit-fast.*

407 *(a) Wash the mouth with warm saline solution (b) Do not use any bit until the injury heals (c) Change or adjust the bit.*

408 *Cracked heels.*

409 *Mud fever.*

410 *Over-reach.*

411 *In the foot.*

412 *Dismount and look for a stone in the hoof.*

413 *Laminitis.*

414 *Navicular.*

415 *Thrush.*

416 *Pedal ostitis.*

417 *Sand crack.*

418 *Yes. Put on a supporting bandage.*

419 *Just in front of the point of the hock.*

420 *Ringbone.*

421 *Splint.*

422 *(a) Common cold or sore throat (b) Virus infection (c) Allergy.*

423 *(a) Vaccination (b) Avoid contact with other horses (c) Avoid drinking or grazing where other horses have been at a show.*

424 *Strangles.*

425 *Vaccination.*

426 *(a) Lungs (b) Larynx.*

427 *(a) Hobdaying (b) Tubing.*

428 *Sweet itch.*

429 *Ringworm.*

430 *(a) In the mane and tail (b) On the lower part of the body.*

431 *(a) Burn bedding, hay and straw (b) Scrub and disinfect stables (c) Wash and disinfect all utensils, tack and clothing.*

432 *Against the back of the hand or bare elbow.*

433 *20 minutes.*

434 *Epsom or common salt.*

435 *Two. One on and one warming up.*

436 *24 hours; longer if there is no poisoning.*

437 *Bran.*

438 *Bruised sole.*

439 *Take his temperature.*

440 *3-6 months.*

441 *Colic.*

442 *Probe it. You could increase the damage.*

443 *Mineral deficiency.*

444 *Protection from cold and extra care in winter.*

THE PONY CLUB

445 There is no minimum age.

446 Under 21 years.

447 Ordinary and Associate.

448 One.

449 Entrance fee and annual subscription.

450 1st November.

451 31st January.

452 17 years.

453 The Pony Club Year Book.

454 Stoneleigh.

455 District Commissioner (DC).

456 The Pony Club Council.

457 Five.

458 Area Representative.

459 19.

460 District Commissioners of the branches in the Area.

461 The British Horse Society (BHS).

462 12 members appointed by the BHS plus all Area representatives.

463 The working rally.

464 (a) Very young ponies. (b) Ponies infirm through age. (c) Ponies ill, thin or lame. (d) Dangerous ponies. (e) Mares about to or recently foaled.

465 The foot can slip through the stirrup iron.

466 Blunt spurs without rowels or sharp edges.

467 *As an occasional visitor or honorary member.*

468 *Protective headgear.*

469 *Only after being seen by a doctor and not on the same day.*

470 *A, H, B, C+, C & D.*

471 *There is also a colour for 'A' Test with honours.*

472 *Purple — 'A' with honours. Blue — 'A'. Orange — 'H'. Red — 'B'. Pink — 'C'+ . Green — 'C' Yellow — 'D'.*

473 *Examiners and DC.*

474 *'D' Test only.*

475 *'B' Test must be held before 'H' Test is attempted.*

476 *Riding and Road Safety; Hunting and Country Lore.*

477 *An official of the Pony Club, 'B' 'Test Examiner, or Visiting Instructor.*

478 *Examiners appointed by the Training Committee.*

479 *3 months.*

480 *Pale blue, gold and purple.*

481 *Dark blue, pale blue and gold.*

482 *The Manual of Horsemanship.*

483 *1929.*

484 *Cottesmore, Craven, Fernie, Ludlow, Old Surrey and Burstow, Shropshire, Sir Watkin William-Wynn's.*

485 *Australia, Canada, Netherlands, USA.*

486 *(a) Associate Membership (b) Recommended by the DC. (c) Holder of 'A', 'H' or 'B' test certificate.*

487 *Visiting Instructor.*

488 *The member's DC or Branch Secretary.*

489 *No money prizes are allowed.*

490 *Blue.*

Competitions and Championships

491 *One-day horse trials called 'The Pony Club Inter-Branch Competition'.*

492 *Horse Trials. Mounted Games. Polo. Tetrathlon. Show Jumping. Dressage.*

493 *Mounted Games and Show Jumping.*

494 *(a) Polo. (b) Mounted Games. (c) Horse Trials. (d) Dressage.*

495 *1949.*

496 *Dressage, show jumping, cross-country.*

497 *Dressage.*

498 *West Norfolk Branch, 1963, 1964, 1965.*

499 *1957.*

500 *Fifteen.*

501 *14.2 hands.*

502 *Five.*

503 *The Horse of the Year Show.*

504 *1959.*

505 *(a) The Jack Gannon. (b) The Rendell.*
(c) The Handley Cross.

506 *1969.*

507 *There are separate boys' and girls' teams.*

508 *Boys only.*

509 *Shooting, swimming, running, riding.*

510 *Shooting and riding.*

511 *1971.*

512 *Four or three, with three to count.*

513 *Table A3.*

514 *1978 (1977 was individual only).*

Riding and Road Safety

515 *The Police or other appointed persons directing traffic.*

516 *All of them.*

517 *Wear reflective clothing and use a safety light.*

518 *Left.*

519 *On the left whether you are leading on foot or from another pony. Place yourself between the led pony and traffic.*

520 *A flashing red light will warn you.*

521 *When the lights go out.*

522 *Ask whether you can pass.*

523 *Never more than two abreast.*

524 *Time your arrival so that you have a clear passage over.*

525 *The road is often slippery from traffic wear.*

526 *Dismount and lead past when the road is clear.*

527 *Near the kerb, edge or gutter, where grit or dirt will provide a safer footing.*

528 *(a) Quit stirrups to anticipate a fall (b) Dismount and lead.*

529 *Fill his feet with grease and carry a hoofpick.*

530 *Make sure that you have third party legal liability insurance.*

531 *(a) A detailed record of exactly what happened.*
(b) A record of what was said by the injured party.
(c) Names of witnesses.

532 *Never admit liability or communicate with anyone making a claim against you.*

533 *Yes on (a) and (b); also on (d) if there are no signs forbidding horses. Never on (c) and (e).*

534 *Say 'Thank you'.*

THE BRITISH HORSE SOCIETY

535 (a) *British Horse Society.*
(b) *Fellow of The British Horse Society.*
(c) *British Horse Society Instructor.*
(d) *British Horse Society Intermediate Instructor.*
(e) *British Horse Society Assistant Instructor.*

536 *The British Equestrian Centre, Stoneleigh.*

537 *1947.*

538 *The National Horse Association of Great Britain, and The Institute of the Horse and Pony Club.*

539 *By Regions and District Representatives.*

540 (a) *Bridleways* (b) *Riding and Road Safety* (c) *Welfare.*

541 (a) *Dressage* (b) *Horse Driving Trials* (c) *Horse Trials* (d) *Long Distance Riding.*

542 (b) *& (e).*

543 *All BHS approved schools display a special sign; you should ask the BHS to send you a list.*

544 *A Local Authority annual licence is needed.*

545 *By enquiry from the BHS, which grades establishments according to standard.*

546 *The BHS includes the scope of each establishment as part of its approval.*

547 *Membership of the BHS and the appropriate BHS Group for the sport concerned.*

548 *The British Equestrian Federation.*

549 *The Royal International Horse Show.*

The Law

550 (a) *Stallions* (b) *Mares with foal at foot.*

551 *Horses registered for racing may be accompanied by any animal which is a stable companion.*

552 *At intervals of not more than 12 hours.*

553 6 feet 6 inches.

554 1911 Protection of Animals Act.

555 The BHS at Stoneleigh, the BHS Regional Welfare Officer, or the local RSPCA Inspector.

556 There is no legislation, but the BHS Code Of Practice has been adopted by the Ministry of Agriculture.

557 Council Offices hold The Definitive Map and Statement of Public Rights of Way.

558 (b), (c) and (d). Field shelters on land of more than one acre may be exempt. You should consult the BHS.

559 (c)

Affiliated Riding Clubs

560 1951.

561 17.

562 If there are at least 12 adult members a junior section can be formed.

563 Grades I, II, III, IV.

564 Holders of the Pony Club 'A' & 'B' Tests are exempt from grades I and II.

565 The Junior Equitation Test.

566 (a) Agriculture and Country Lore (b) Saddlery (c) The Foot and Shoeing (d) Keeping a Pony or Horse at Grass (e) Grooming and Rugging (f) Riding and Road Sense.

567 (a) Team Dressage (b) Prix Caprilli (c) Pair Dressage (d) Equitation Jumping (e) Team Show Jumping (f) Horse Trials.

568 The Riding Club Team Class at the Royal International Horse Show. The Riding Club Quadrille at the Horse of the Year Show.

SPORTS AND PASTIMES

Hunting

569 *1st November.*

570 *The field.*

571 *The Field Master.*

572 *In couples.*

573 *The amount paid by a non-subscriber for a day's hunting.*

574 *The Master. Say 'Good morning Master'.*

575 *(a) Gorse, wood or growth in which a fox may be found.*
(b) The scent trail of the hunted fox.
(c) When the scent is weak either because of ground
conditions or because the fox is far ahead of hounds.
(d) When hounds hunt in the opposite direction taken
by the fox.
(e) A fox turned from the direction in which he is going by
someone in front of him.
(f) A tiring fox.
(g) A fox's head.
(h) A fox's tail.
(i) Foot of fox, hare or hound.
(j) Two foxes.
(k) A fox's lair.

576 *(a) Stern.*
(b) A couple.
(c) Kennels.
(d) Lodges.
(e) Benches.
(f) Yard.
(g) 'All on'.

577 *Harrier, beagle, basset.*

578 *(a) The cry of the pack when they scent their quarry.*
(b) Giving tongue in kennel.
(c) Giving tongue over a place where a fox has gone to ground.

579 *To communicate with his hounds and with the field.*

580 *(a) When hounds temporarily lose the scent.*
(b) Applies to any animal of a different species to that which is hunted.
(c) Any scent which obliterates the scent of the quarry.
(d) To come on a fox suddenly and kill it.
(e) A fox which sets a straight course.

581 *'Ware wire'.*

582 *A shout or yell by someone who has seen a fox.*

583 *Whippers-in. If more than one they are called First or Second Whipper-in.*

584 *Freshly seeded land which must be ridden round, not crossed.*

585 *(a) A meet held at a private house.*
(b) A meet when two packs combine under the huntsman of one of them.
(c) A meet in the country of another hunt by invitation of that hunt.

586 *They are major hound shows.*

587 *(a) To educate young hounds (b) To locate and assess the fox population after the breeding season (c) To scatter the young adult foxes (d) To reduce the number of young adult foxes to that which the local countryside can support (e) To complete the fitness training of hounds and horses.*

588 *(b).*

589 *(d).*

590 *(b).*

591 *(a).*

592 *(c).*

593 *(a).*

594 *(d).*

595 *(d).*

596 *'Good Night'.*

Horse Trials

597 (a) *1948.*
      (b) *1949.*
      (c) *Badminton.*
      (d) *The 10th Duke of Beaufort.*
      (e) *John Shedden on Goldon Willow.*

598 *Great Auclum.*

599 *Dressage.*

600 *Roads and tracks, steeplechase and cross-country.*

601 *1.05m (3ft 6ins).*

602 *15 hands.*

603 *An enclosure from which horses are started on the cross-country phase.*

604 *Jack Le Goff, former USA team trainer.*

605 (a) *Badminton.*
      (b) *Haras du Pin.*
      (c) *Helsinki — 'Helsinki steps'.*

606 (a) *Chatsworth* (b) *Burghley* (c) *Tidworth* (d) *Badminton.*

607 *1956 — Stockholm.*

608 *1972 — Munich. Richard Meade on Lauriston.*

609 *The owner of the horse which wins most points in a season.*

610 (a) *Lt-Col Frank Weldon* (b) *Sheila Willcox; (c), (d) and (e) Lucinda Prior-Palmer/Lucinda Green.*

611 *Gurgle the Greek, ridden by Rachel Baylis.*

612 *Lucinda and David Green for Great Britain and Australia.*

Dressage

613 *40m×20m.*

614 *60m×20m.*

615 *C,M,B,F,A,K,E,H.*

616 *A.*

617 *X.*

618 *R,S,V,P,I,L.*

619 *Six.*

620 *Mrs Joan Gold on Gay Gordon.*

621 Mrs Jennie Loriston-Clarke on Dutch Courage.

622 William Cavendish, Duke of Newcastle (1592-1676).

623 La Guérinière.

Show Jumping

624 British Show Jumping Association.

625 1925.

626 A,B, & C.

627 JA & JC.

628 14.2 Hands.

629 16.

630 From age 13 to 16 as Junior Associate Members.

631 (a) 7m (23ft) (b) 10m (33ft).

632 18.25m (60ft).

633 Horses jump off a shorter stride in the smaller ring.

634 (a) Table C (b) Table A5.

635 275m (301 yds), 300m (328 yds), 320m (360 yds), 350m (383 yds), 400m (436 yds) per minute.

636 The time limit is twice the time allowed.

637 When water has two or more poles over it, it is judged as a normal obstacle.

638 Puissance.

639 The Judge.

640 Elimination in each case.

641 When the rider has remounted.

642 1866 at a show in Paris.

643 The Horse of the Year Show.

644 Hickstead.

645 Harvey Smith.

646 (a) Royal International (b) Great Yorkshire (c) Dublin.

647 Queen Elizabeth II Cup.

648 Foxhunter.

649 Four members, each jumping two rounds.

650 Prince Philip Trophy.

Polo

651 Four.

652 No 4.

653 Chukkas.

654 Six.

655 (a) 10, (b) Minus 2.

656 The player following the ball on its exact line.

657 There is no off-side.

658 Players may only play right-handed.

659 30 yds (27m); 40 yds (36m); 60 yds (54m).

660 Bandages or boots on all four legs.

661 300 yds×200 yds.

662 8yds (7m).

663 The Hurlingham Polo Association.

Driving

664 Presentation, dressage, marathon and obstacle driving.

665 (a) Presentation and dressage — Competition A.
(b) Marathon — Competition B (c) Obstacle Driving —
Competition C.

666 All three.

667 The cleanliness and general condition of horses, harness and
vehicle.

668 No. A different vehicle can be used for the marathon.

669 No. A reserve horse may be used as laid down in the rules.

670 Ponies must be under 148cm (14.2¼ hands).

671 (a) A pair (b) Tandem (c) Four-in-hand.

672 There is a minimum weight for the marathon.

673 They may ride on one only.

674 Only the driver may handle all three on penalty of
elimination.

675 (a) 100m×40m (c) 80m×40m.

676 They are the same.

Long Distance Riding

677 *(a) Horsemastership (b) Fitness of horse and rider (c) Judgement of pace.*

678 *Two.*

679 *Day 1 — 50 miles (80km). Day 2 — 25 miles (40km).*

680 *40 miles (64km).*

681 *8mph without penalties.*

682 *The veterinary inspection.*

683 *100 miles. 50 miles on each of two days.*

684 *On time. The fastest time without penalties wins.*

Showing

685 *Working Hunter Pony.*

686 *They are 2ins higher in each class. WHP limits are 13 hands, 14 hands, 15 hands. Ridden pony are 12.2 hands, 13.2 hands, 14.2 hands.*

687 *(a) One part requires jumping a course of natural fences; the other requires showing.*
(b) The same rider must do both parts using the same tack.

688 *Jodhpurs, collar and tie, hat, coat, leather-covered cane.*

689 *(a) 11.2 and 12.2 hands (c) To the cavesson noseband (c) Snaffle.*

690 *Walk and trot.*

691 *All the native breeds — Connemara, Dale, Dartmoor, Exmoor, Fell, Highland, New Forest, Shetland, Welsh.*

692 *(a) A,B,C & D. (b) Section D.*

693 *Ridden pony classes.*

694 *Breeding and young stock.*

695 *Heavyweight, middleweight, lightweight, ladies', and small hunter.*

696 *Small hunter, small hack, and ladies' hack.*

Racing

697 *The Jockey Club.*

698 *Steeplechases.*

699 *Point-to-Point Races.*

700 *2 years.*

701 *2000 Guineas, 1000 Guineas, Derby, Oaks, St Leger.*

702 *1½ miles.*

703 *St Leger.*

704 *Four wins by Sceptre in 1902. She was also 4th in the Derby.*

705 *Lester Piggott.*

706 *(d) Formerly held by Frank Buckle.*

707 *They are made of growing thorn; others are made of cut birch.*

708 *Plain fence, open ditch, water jump.*

709 *Short head, head, neck, ½ length, ¾ length, length, distance.*

710 *(a) Red Rum (b) The Tetrarch (c) Eclipse (d) Shergar.*

711 *(a) Aintree, Liverpool (b) Epsom (c)Sandown Park (d) Ascot (e) Kempton Park (f) Newmarket.*

712 *(a) Newmarket (b) Aintree (c) Epsom (d) Sandown Park. (e) Newmarket (f) Chester (g) Ascot(h) York (i) Aintree.*

713 *(a) Fred Archer (b) Steve Donoghue (c) Harry Wragg (d) Willie Shoemaker, USA (e) Lester Piggott.*

714 *(a) Either a light racing shoe or a race in which the prize money is guaranteed (b) The start or finish of of a race (c) Starting stalls used in flat racing (d) Slang for a horse dishonestly substituted for another (e) The area in which bets are laid, also the bookmakers who work there (f) Used at jumping meetings or when no stalls are available to start a race. They are strung across the course and raised by the starter (g) The coloured jacket worn by a flat race jockey (h) A race in which only a single runner takes part.*

715 *(a) Won first-ever ladies race (Kempton Park 1972). Was also first champion lady jockey (b) First woman to train a Grand National winner (1983), first woman to train a Cheltenham Gold Cup winner (1984) (c) First woman to win a National Hunt race (Stratford 1976) (d) First woman to complete the Grand National course (1983) (e) First woman to win a National Hunt race as a professional (1978).*

716 *They were all trained by Michael Dickinson.*

717 (a) *Lincoln Handicap and Grand National.*
(b) *Cesarewitch and Cambridgeshire.*

718 (a) *Official programme for a race meeting* (b) *Railed enclosure where the horses are paraded and mounted before a race.*
(c) *Slang term for an amateur rider on the flat. Also applied to amateur flat races* (d) *A person permitted to train under National Hunt rules for their immediate family only.*

719 (a) *Horses racing or exercising beside each other are 'upsides'*
(b) *When a horse is persuaded to take off too early at a fence because he is half a length behind the horse next to him.*

720 *Unplaced (not in the first three).*

721 *Queen Anne.*

722 *Sir Gordon Richards.*

723 *Fred Winter.*

724 *Vincent O'Brien.*

725 *Blue.*

SOME GENERAL QUESTIONS

The 'Equine Connection'

726 Poisonous plants.

727 Face markings.

728 Mucking-out tools.

729 Farrier's tools.

730 Girths.

731 Should all be in the medicine cupboard.

732 Diseases and afflictions of the skin.

733 German breeds of horse.

734 Parts of the saddle.

735 John Peel's hounds.

736 Materials used to make the mouthpieces of bits.

737 Bits (gag, pelham, snaffle, snaffle).

738 'Airs above the Ground' or High School movements.

739 Carriages.

740 Root vegetables relished by horses.

741 All suitable for feeding horses (and their owners!)

742 Grasses found in hay.

743 Used to make numnahs.

744 Grooming.

745 Spavins.

746 The horses of William Cody (Buffalo Bill).

747 *Bits (gag, gag, snaffle, pelham).*

748 *The classic races of the USA.*

749 *Famous runs (Beaufort, Heythrop, Pytchley, Quorn).*

750 *Well known coverts or finds (Belvoir, Whaddon Chase, Fernie, Quantock).*

751 *The six breeding lines of Lipizzaners.*

752 *Parts of an anvil.*

753 *Surgical shoes.*

754 *The horses from whom all Thoroughbreds are descended.*

755 *Parts of a horseshoe nail.*

Over the Seas and Far Away

756 *Africa.*

757 *Kentucky.*

758 *Austria.*

759 *Ireland.*

760 *Bronco and mustang.*

761 *Brumby.*

762 *Cadre Noir.*

763 *(a) Canada (b) USA (c) South Africa (d) Czechoslovakia (e) USA (f) Australia (g) France.*

764 *The Morgan Horse.*

765 *Siena.*

766 *(a) Chestnut (b) Piebald or Skewbald.*

767 *The Camargue in Southern France.*

768 *Quarter horse.*

769 *By Pony Express.*

770 *Trakehner.*

771 *Pig-sticking in India.*

772 *Argentina.*

773 *The wild horse in Central Asia.*

774 *Australia. The Roycroft family of father and two sons.*

775 *Acey-deucey.*

Take Your Pick

776	(a).	**794**	(a).
777	(c).	**795**	(b).
778	(b).	**796**	(c).
779	(c).	**797**	(b).
780	(b).	**798**	(a).
781	(d).	**799**	(a).
782	(c).	**800**	(b).
783	(d).	**801**	(a).
784	(b).	**802**	(c).
785	(c).	**803**	(a).
786	(b).	**804**	(a).
787	(c).	**805**	(b).
788	(d).	**806**	(b).
789	(d).	**807**	(d).
790	(c).	**808**	(d).
791	(d).	**809**	(b).
792	(d).	**810**	(c).
793	(b).		

A Visit to the Zoo?

811 *Ewe neck.*

812 *Goose rump.*

813 *Herring gutted or waspy.*

814 *Cow hocks.*

815 *Cock-throttled.*

816 *Parrot mouth.*

817 *Flea bitten.*

818 *Donkey foot.*

819 *Pigeon toes.*

820 *Pig eye.*

821 *Calf knee.*

822 *Roach back.*

823 *Cat hairs.*

824 *Bull neck.*

825 *Swan neck.*

826 *Peacocky.*

827 *Wolf teeth.*

828 *Ermine marks.*

829 *Zebra stripes.*

830 *Rat tail.*

831 *Elk lip.*

832 *Oyster feet.*

833 *Leopard marking.*

834 *Salmon marks.*

835 *Serpent tail.*

836 *Ram headed.*

837 *Toad eye.*

838 *A dog.*

839 *Daisy cutter.*

840 *Bird eyed.*

Odd One Out

841 *Martingales. (d) A noseband.*

842 *British native breeds. (c) American breed.*

843 *Boots worn by the horse. (b) Worn by the rider.*

844 *Body clips. (b) A clipped mane.*

845 *Bedding. (d) Palatable and therefore the least suitable straw.*

846 *Horse rugs. (c) A noseband.*

847 *Used to keep the saddle in place. (a) Used to influence head carriage.*

848 *Grooming brushes. (c) Curry comb.*

849 *Natural aids. (c) Artificial aid.*

850 *Bandages. (a).*

851 *Saddle injuries. (b) Usually caused by lack of bedding.*

852 *Stable vices. (c) Stubborn and unwilling to go forward.*

853 *French breeds. (a) Spanish.*

854   Hock injuries. (b) Fetlock swelling.

855   Parts of the body shared by both man and horse. (c) The horse's knee is the equivalent.

856   Diseases of the foot. (a) Digestive disorder.

857   Good paddock fencing materials. (d) Unsuitable for horses.

858   Parts of the shoe. (c) A frame around the neck fitted to prevent tearing bandages and biting wounds.

859   Boots. (b)

860   Succulent horse feeds. (a) A dry feed.

861   Equestrian artists. (d) Equestrian author.

862   Racecourses under both rules. (b) National Hunt only.

863   Corrective shoes. (a) Assurance of soundness given to a purchaser.

864   All different names for the same disease except (d).

865   Three intestinal worms. (a) Ringworm is a fungal skin disease.

Double Meanings

866   (a) Colour.
(b) Bony growth on the inside of the leg.

867   (a) Part of the face around the mouth and nostrils.
(b) A guard to prevent a horse from eating or biting.

868   (a) A type of bit.
(b) A thickening of the ligament below the hock.

869   (a) To knock one leg with another.
(b) A grooming article.
(c) A fox's tail.
(d) A birch fence.

870   (a) To lose a shoe.
(b) A horse unable to get up in its stable.
(c) To throw a horse to the ground, usually for veterinary purposes.
(d) To get rid of an inferior or unsuitable horse.
(e) An effort by hounds to recover the scent.

871   (a) The side of the face.
(b) The straight side part of some bits.
(c) Part of the bridle.

872 (a) *A horse which has lost condition.*
    (b) *To pull the stirrup irons to the top of the leathers.*
    (c) *To show off a horse in hand.*
    (d) *To increase fraudulently the bidding at a horse auction.*

873 (a) *A horse which takes a strong hold is said to pull.*
    (b) *To thin the mane or tail.*
    (c) *To prevent a horse from winning a race.*

874 (a) *Measurement around the leg below the knee.*
    (b) *Used for polishing calf-leather boots.*
    (c) *Frost-bound ground is said to have 'bone' in it.*

875 (a) *A horse-breeding establishment.*
    (b) *A fitting screwed into a shoe to prevent slipping.*

876 (a) *An artificial aid.*
    (b) *Short for whipper-in.*
    (c) *An intestinal worm.*

877 (a) *Part of a horse.*
    (b) *A distance between horses at the finish of a race.*
    (c) *That part of a spur which projects to the rear.*

878 (a) *The condition of the ground.*
    (b) *The way in which a horse is performing.*

879 (a) *The place where a farrier works.*
    (b) *To strike a foreshoe with a hind.*

880 (a) *A piece of leather.*
    (b) *A grooming action.*

881 (a) *To remove the hair of the coat.*
    (b) *Part of a horse shoe.*

882 (a) *Part of horse.*
    (b) *To mount an unbroken horse for the first time.*
    (c) *To rein back.*
    (d) *To place a bet on a horse.*

883 (a) *To put a horse loose in a field.*
    (b) *A two or four wheeled vehicle.*
    (c) *The general appearance of horse, rider and any equipage.*

884 (a) *A strap to secure the saddle.*
    (b) *That part of the horse which is around the body behind the elbows.*

885 (a) *To braid the mane or tail.*
    (b) *Faulty action with crossing legs.*

886 (a) *Part of the jaw between incisors and molars.*
    (b) *Metal strips on the saddle to which stirrup leathers are attached.*

(c) *Part of harness to which the leaders' traces are attached.*
(d) *Part of the foot.*
(e) *A name for the cheek piece on a curb bit.*

887   (a) *An injury to the coronet.*
(b) *The rubber insert on a stirrup iron.*

888   (a) *Worn on the head.*
(b) *The fee for a day's hunting.*

889   (a) *A race rider.*
(b) *A spot of black, greasy dirt on a saddle.*
(c) *A metal slide to guide the foot into a riding boot.*

890   (a) *A horse's throat.*
(b) *The groove between the padding of a saddle to accommodate the spine.*
(c) *The lower end of a horse collar.*

891   (a) *Oats or barley when used as a feed.*
(b) *A bruising of the sole near the heel.*

892   (a) *Substance of the wall of the hoof.*
(b) *Blown by a huntsman or coachman.*

893   (a) *To gallop out of control.*
(b) *To eat quickly and greedily.*
(c) *A stable door fastening.*
(d) *To flush a fox from a hole, drain or earth.*

894   (a) *To educate a young horse.*
(b) *An unasked-for change of gait: eg, canter during trot.*
(c) *When a fox leaves covert.*

895   (a) *A grass field into which horses are turned out.*
(b) *A railed enclosure used to parade horses before a race.*

896   (a) *Rosettes — to be 'in the ribbons'.*
(b) *A driving term for reins.*

897   (a) *Acceptance of the bit.*
(b) *A stage after entry and before declaration of a race.*

898   (a) *Long hair on the fetlocks.*
(b) *The waving of a hound's stern as it picks up the scent.*

899   (a) *Worn by the rider.*
(b) *Worn by the horse.*
(c) *The luggage compartment of a coach.*
(d) *To urge a horse to greater speed.*

900   (a) *A foodstuff.*
(b) *Black centres of the incisor teeth.*

Books, Poems and Pictures

901 *King Richard III.*

902 *Banbury Cross.*

903 *Put Humpty-Dumpty together again.*

904 *John Gilpin (William Cowper).*

905 *Whyte-Melville in* The Good Grey Mare.

906 *Paul Revere (Longfellow).*

907 *Joris and Dirck (Robert Browning).*

908 *Centaur.*

909 *(a) Apollo (b) Mahomet (c) Gandalf (*The Lord of the Rings *by Tolkien).*

910 *(a) King Arthur (b) Sir Guyon (*Faerie Queen *by Spencer).*

911 *Bayard.*

912 *Babieca.*

913 *White (*Revelations XIX, v XI*).*

914 *Caligula. The horse was Incitatus.*

915 *Alexander the Great.*

916 *It whinnied before those of his rivals.*

917 *Winnie.*

918 *Polo (Kipling)*

919 *Right Royal (Masefield).*

920 *Silver Blaze (Conan Doyle).*

921 *The Cock and Pie (*Reynard the Fox *by Masefield).*

922 *Frou-Frou (*Anna Karenina *by Leo Tolstoy).*

923 *The trilogy* Experiences of an Irish RM *(Somerville and Ross).*

924 *It died from being overfed (Hilaire Belloc).*

925 *(a) Enid Bagnold (b) John Steinbeck (c) Mary O'Hara (d) Edward Lear (e) Monica Edwards (f) Golden Gorse.*

926 Hunter Trials *by John Betjeman.*

927 The Sport of Queens.

928 *(a) John Jorrocks (b) Lord Scamperdale (c) Jack Spraggon (d) Soapey Sponge (e) Facey Romford (f) Jogglebury Crowdy (g) James Pigg (h) Benjamin Brady.*

929 The Whipper-in *by R.E. Egerton-Warburton.*

930 (a) ..*make it drink.* (b) ..*mouth.* (c) ..*as a horse.* (d) ..*in the mouth.* (e) ..*stumbles.* (f) ..*to horse ....*

931 *The White Horse of the White Horse Vale.*

932 *'The horse was lost;'*

933 *'Three jolly gentlemen in coats of red'* (The Huntsmen *by Walter de la Mare).*

934 *The horses were the 'Houyhnhnms', the humans 'Yahoos'.*

935 *Rosinante.*

936 *Stubbs.*

937 *Toulouse-Lautrec.*

938 *China (Eastern Han AD 25-222).*

939 *Degas.*

940 *George Stubbs.*

941 *Lady Elizabeth Butler.*

942 *J.F. Herring, Senior.*

943 *Theodore Gericault.*

944 *Sir Alfred Munnings.*

945 *Snaffles.*

The Numbers Game

946 *64.*

947 *2.*

948 *3.*

949 *7.*

950 *4.*

951 *10.*

952 *8.*

953 *24.*

954 *5.*

955 *6 in a row.*

956 *Never.*

957 *4.*

958 *8.*

959 *4.*

960 *8. Bill Brewer, Jan Stewer, Peter Gurney, Peter Davey, Dan'l Whiddon, Harry Hawk, Old Uncle Tom Cobbleigh, and the narrator.*

The End of the Road

961 (a) *Riding for the Disabled Association.*
(b) *Fédération Equestre Internationale.*
(c) *Concours Complet Internationale Officiel*
(Three-Day Event).
(d) *Concours de Dressage Internationale Officiel (Dressage).*
(e) *Concours de Saut d' Obstacles Internationale Officiel*
(Show Jumping).

962 *A brood mare.*

963 *On corner incisor teeth at 10 years.*

964 *Tampering with a horse's teeth to disguise its age.*

965 *The Alcock Arabian.*

966 *1912 (Stockholm).*

967 (d) *6 gallons.*

968 *80%.*

969 *Silver and Gold.*

970 *'C' Test for Silver. 'B' Test for Gold.*

971 *Suffolk Punch.*

972 *In 1803 from Ipswich to Nacton.*

973 *A circus horse whose back is rubbed with resin to provide a grip.*

974 *Left hand to left hand.*

975 (a) *15.1 hands* (b) *14.2 hands.*

976 *Pacing or ambling.*

977 *In a forge. The fireman makes and fits the shoes; the doorman prepares the feet and nails the shoes on.*

978 *Tschiffely rode from Buenos Aires to Washington DC; 10,000 miles in 2½ years.*

979 (a) *Black Bess.*
(b) *Black Beauty.*
(c) *Black Saladin.*
(d) *Black Agnes.*
(e) *Black Allan.*

980 *St Christopher.*